What People Are Saying
The Definitive Guide to the Prophetic...

"Joni Ames has done an outstanding presentation of proper use of prophetic ministry and other supernatural experiences in the church. I have a great concern for integrity and proper principles being practiced in the prophetic ministry. The prophetic movement was birthed at our International Prophets Conference in 1988. God supernaturally challenged me to take a fathering role in the movement. Being a church historian and restoration minister, I knew that foundational guidelines had to be established immediately to keep the prophetic in biblical order. Bless you, Joni, for continuing to promote the prophetic ministry with integrity, wisdom, and proper guidelines."

—*Dr. Bill Hamon*
Author
Bishop, Christian International Ministries' Apostolic Global Network

"It seems tedious sometimes to find a prophet who has time to answer questions about his or her gifting. It's even more tedious to find one who has a passion to anoint a younger prophet in his or her place, to be a 'servant in training,' as Elijah did with Elisha. This book and this person speaks powerfully to that need. For years, Joni Ames has gone about her quiet, sweet, unassuming ways, speaking powerfully into our culture. She now takes a bold step into the future to advocate and apply the biblical pattern of unity—the father/son paradigm. Every believer will do well to read and heed this strategic book."

—*Jack Taylor*
Dimensions Ministries

"From time to time in the prophetic movement, it becomes important to have a new work available for those seeking to better hear God's voice. Joni Ames's new book, *The Definitive Guide to the Prophetic, is* that book. Every few years, new language comes into use and greater understandings are arrived at, to help young or fresh prophetic voices know 'how do I get from where I am to being used by God in prophesying to others?' Again, *this is that book*. Not only is it a great stand-alone book, but I also see it being used in classrooms and home groups for discussions on how to manage and understand God's emerging prophetic voices in the body of Christ!"

—*Steve Shultz*
President, The Elijah List

"Joni Ames is a solid prophetic voice in the church today. Now, in *The Definitive Guide to the Prophetic*, she shares everything she has learned through her years of walking with the Lord and operating as a prophet."

—*Dr. Roberts Liardon*
Roberts Liardon Ministries
Embassy International Church

"My wife, Romy, and I have known Joni Ames for over twenty years. In that time, she has consistently spoken into our lives with accurate prophetic revelation and love. This book is filled with gems of her wisdom for anyone interested in growing in prophetic ministry. Joni has spent many years traveling the country, sharing her gifts with many thousands of believers. In this book, she teaches on character, discernment, sanctification, forgiveness, healing, angels and demons, and many more subjects to help you in your prophetic walk. You won't be able to put the book down."

—*Steven Zarit*
Former general manager/vice president
Vineyard Ministries International (1986–1994)

"*The Definitive Guide to the Prophetic* gives everyone the chance to sit down with Joni Ames, a respected and anointed prophetic minister, and learn what she has to impart about this vital ministry. I've known Joni for over two decades, and I can vouch for her character and integrity. No matter your level of knowledge and experience—from new Christian to seasoned saint—there is much to be gleaned from this excellent book."

—*Robert Whitlow*
Filmmaker and best-selling author of fifteen legal thrillers, including *Mountain Top*

"Joni Ames radiates her love of the Lord, His purposes and truth, through her laser-sharp prophetic insight. In this season of increasing darkness, fake news, and media mind-control, we all need sharper discernment. Joni is a wise master-builder in the arena of discerning of the times and spirits, and teaching all the Lord desires His body to know about moving in the Holy Spirit. Joni's voice and writing is clear, articulate, refreshing, and thorough, full of wisdom and light. We love her prayers at the end of each chapter, and the many practical applications. She will activate within you that 'holy fire' to seek and find the Lord, to know His voice, and to search out His many treasures awaiting your discovery."

—*Jorge Parrott, PhD*
Director, Eagle Missions at MorningStar
President, MorningStar University College of Theology

THE
DEFINITIVE GUIDE
TO THE
PROPHETIC

GOD'S GIFT FOR YOU AND THE CHURCH

JONI AMES

WHITAKER
HOUSE

The Definitive Guide to the Prophetic:
God's Gift for You and the Church

Joni Ames
P.O. Box 36667
Rock Hill, SC 29732
JoniAmes.com
JoniAmes@aol.com

ISBN: 978-1-64123-150-3
eBook ISBN: 978-1-64123-151-0
Printed in the United States of America
© 2018 by Joni Ames

Whitaker House
1030 Hunt Valley Circle
New Kensington, PA 15068
www.whitakerhouse.com

Library of Congress Cataloging-in-Publication Data (Pending)

1 2 3 4 5 6 7 8 9 10 11 **W** 25 24 23 22 21 20 19 18

ACKNOWLEDGMENTS

It is with a grateful heart that I give honor to those who have impacted my life, personally and spiritually. Thank you also to those who have helped me pull this book together and make it happen, after twenty-two years in the making.

First of all, my thanks to my children, Jennifer and CJ; my son-in-law, Maynard; and my grandchildren, Zachary, Megan, and Brooke, who have been my lifeline of love and encouragement through everything.

Then, in alphabetical order, my thanks to those who have been the greatest influence in my prophetic walk:

Mike Bickle, whom God used to save my life, literally, in the early days of my ministry. God also used him to remind me that prayer, along with a right relationship with God, is the number one priority, and the road to Shiloh.

Paul Cain, who allowed me to attend his Shiloh retreat and sit at his feet to learn from a true prophetic master. His book with R. T. Kendall, *The Word and the Spirit*, touched and encouraged me at a crucial time in my life.

Chuck Flynn, now deceased, who, in 1989, gave me the most incredible and accurate prophetic word of my life, one that outlined my calling in detail. I didn't believe it then, but every part of it has come to pass.

James W. Goll, who has been a constant friend and encourager, as well as the catalyst for helping me become a published author. Prophet Bob

Jones gifted me with James' book *The Seer*, to help me better understand who God made me to be.

Michal Ann Goll, my precious and dear friend, now gone to be with the Lord, whose life and encouragement I will forever hold dear.

Bishop Bill Hamon, whose ministry challenged and forever changed the way I prophesied.

Prophet Bob Jones (now deceased), my prophetic papa, who allowed me the privilege and honor of being his daughter, and part of his personal mentoring group in his home for five years.

Deborah Joyner, my dear friend and editor, who spent many hours editing and teaching me the ins and outs of writing a book.

Rick Joyner, my friend and main prophetic mentor, whom I met in 1990 and for whom I worked as his first secretary, and have been a part of MorningStar ever since. It was through his leadership and encouragement that I stepped out into ministry.

Rev. Gene Kennett (and his wife, Shirley, now deceased) of Interfaith Worship Center, in Erie, Pennsylvania (my original home church). They saved my life.

Steve Thompson, the first one who trained and activated so many of us to hear from God and minister to others on prophetic teams in the early days of MorningStar.

And, last but not least, thank you to all who have spoken prophetically into my life and have given me the courage to walk in the ministry that God has called me to do.

Thank you to the pastors and leaders who have trusted and allowed me the awesome privilege and honor of ministering to them and their groups over the past twenty-plus years.

Thank you to the women who were a part of my "Women's Prophetic Destiny" conferences, for sharing in the adventure.

Thank you to those who helped proofread and refine my book: Debbi Carlson, Michael Jancaterino, Doug Lee, Robin Rowan, Ron Wallace, and Robert Whitlow.

CONTENTS

FOREWORD

I am always on the lookout for the triple threat. I am not just looking for those who have the potential to carry the double. No, I have my eyes peeled for the triple threat—an individual who is adept in three different fields of activity, all at the same time.

In professional football, a triple threat is a player who excels at running, kicking, and passing. These players are always the top draft picks. When it comes to Major League Baseball, there is what is called the Triple Crown winner—the rare player who leads the league in offensive statistics in runs batted in, batting average, and home runs in a single season. Then, there's the world of horse racing, in which the illustrious Triple Crown winner must place first in the biggest three races: the Kentucky Derby, the Preakness Stakes, and the Belmont Stakes.

I wonder if a similar title exists in Christian ministry. If so, I know it is as rare as the triple threats mentioned in the sports arena. In Christian ministry, a triple treat would be a dedicated leader who has an excellent reputation in three distinct areas: gifting, character, and mentoring. Some leaders have extraordinary gifting and are greatly anointed by the Holy Spirit but fall short in character to carry their gift. Some shine in the area of ethical character but are rather "flat" in the things of the Spirit. A few might be dedicated to the task of gathering others around them, only to eventually find out that they have been attempting to fill a hole of significance in their own lives. It seems that potholes are everywhere. But is that really the case?

I have often stated that my personal goal in ministry is to "go for the double"—to pursue a combination anointing of character with an abundance of the fruit of the Spirit to carry the calling that involves the gifts of the Spirit. While that is a noble aim, it is no longer what I am striving for in my own life, nor is it a goal I set for anyone else. Now that I am getting older in chronological age, I am choosing to pursue a combination of these three things: gifts, fruit, and multiplication!

Why, in this foreword to a book written by a friend of mine, am I talking about being a triple threat? Good question! As I have prayed and meditated upon the life and ministry of Joni Ames, knowing this is her inaugural book to be presented to the body of Christ, I wanted to state something out of the ordinary about this extraordinary person.

Joni loves the cross of the Lord Jesus Christ. She believes in the supernatural dimensions of the Holy Spirit, but in a "no-nonsense" manner. She is committed to personal integrity, accountability, and humility. Joni is also a champion for the little guy and for the down-and-out. She is as comfortable doing a meeting in a home as she is in addressing a large audience at a major conference. She loves church pastors, and she believes that the fivefold ministry offices can complement one another; the prophetic need not be in competition with pastoral authority.

Over the years, I have had the great honor of walking with some of the best trainers and equippers in various realms of ministry. As a personal friend, a trusted confidant, and one who has his eyes open for the triple threat, I have the great honor of commending to you the gift, the character, and the mentoring grace of Joni Faith Ames.

May you be edified, exhorted, and comforted as you glean wisdom from these pages so that you, too, may join the prophetic company of modern-day Simeons and Annas on the rise in this generation.

Blessings to you!

—*James W. Goll*
Founder, God Encounters Ministries
Internationally sought speaker, author, and communications trainer

PREFACE

The purpose of this book is to provide a biblical explanation—one that is also clear, concise, and practical—of the operation and function of personal prophetic ministry in the church today. It is my goal for this book to act as a teacher, mentor, and counseling tool to help prophetic people understand themselves and their gifting, and to grow and mature in that gifting. I also desire to help pastors and other church leaders understand, acknowledge, discern, and train the prophetic community within the bodies of believers that they lead.

In addition, my hope is that this book will help debunk some of the prevailing myths and falsehoods surrounding the prophetic, and that it will bring a greater level of maturity and confidence to those seeking to develop their own revelatory gifts.

Over the course of many years, I have asked people all over the world to submit to me the topics they would like to see covered in this book. I have endeavored to honor every suggestion I received.

May this book help prophetic people to realize their place, value, and purpose in the kingdom of God upon the earth today, and to fulfill that purpose.

INTRODUCTION:
THE JOURNEY BEGINS

God has chosen the foolish things of the world to put to shame the
wise, and God has chosen the weak things of the world to put to
shame the things which are mighty; and the base things of the world
and the things which are despised God has chosen, and the things
which are not, to bring to nothing the things that are, that no flesh
should glory in His presence. But of Him you are in Christ Jesus,
who became for us wisdom from God—and righteousness and
sanctification and redemption—that, as it is written,
"He who glories, let him glory in the LORD."
—1 Corinthians 1:27–31

Prophecy has the power to change someone, literally, into another person. (See 1 Samuel 10:6.) I'm not the woman I used to be. Through the voices of those who offered me prophetic encouragement, God reached into my shy, backward world and transformed it forever.

When you have a call of God on your life, you may have to fight for it, possibly even as you come into the world. You may have entered the world through a difficult birth, or you may have grown up in a dysfunctional home environment. Tragedies, drama, and trauma may litter your path. Perhaps, even as a child, you experienced nightmares or demonic visitations. Perhaps you can't explain it, but you just "know" certain things. You pick up on an unscrupulous person of whom everyone else thinks the world. You may sense who is calling on the phone or knocking at the door. You may feel in your spirit that something is wrong or amiss before an unfortunate event takes place. At times, you may feel downright crazy.

If the above is true of you, then misunderstanding, misinterpretation, miscommunication, false accusation, and even rejection may seem to "come after" you. Take heart! This is what Jesus said:

> *Blessed are you when they revile and persecute you, and say all kinds of evil against you falsely for My sake. Rejoice and be exceedingly glad, for great is your reward in heaven, for so they persecuted the prophets who were before you.* (Matthew 5:11–12)

The Bible promises a coming restoration of all things. (See Acts 3:21.) Meanwhile, the Lord offers to us restoration of the years the locusts have eaten. (See Joel 2:25.) God is in the restoration business.

No matter what season of life you find yourself in, it's never too late to step into the fullness of God's gifts and everything that He has for you. Receive it and live it, because you can.

Let's get started!

1

PROPHECY AS A FOUNDATIONAL FIVEFOLD MINISTRY

The term *fivefold ministry* refers to the church-related roles of apostle, prophet, evangelist, pastor, and teacher. (See Ephesians 4:11.) The job of those who serve in any of these five roles is to train and equip the body of Christ. The entire passage of Ephesians 4:11–16 is the very foundation of the conviction that believers can be inhabited by the Holy Spirit, and that the gifts of the Holy Spirit, as outlined in 1 Corinthians 12:8–10, are still relevant for the church today.

Earlier on in his letter to the Ephesians, the apostle Paul laid out the basis of this belief:

> *Having been built on the foundation for the apostles and prophets, Jesus Christ Himself being the chief cornerstone, in whom the whole building, being fitted together, grows into a holy temple in the Lord, in whom you also are being built together for a dwelling place of God in the Spirit.* (Ephesians 2:20–22)

Thankfully, the church still has available to it the same power for which Jesus paid the price of His blood. And He deserves to get that which He paid for.

Some churches teach that both the fivefold ministry and the gifts of the Spirit are no longer in existence. It is the opinion of those who subscribe to this view that the fivefold offices and gifts of the Holy Spirit—even the

17

gift of healing—passed away with the death of the apostles. However, Ephesians 4:11–16 clearly contradicts such a belief.

The fivefold ministry is God's list of equippers. *"He Himself gave some to be apostles, some prophets, some evangelists, and some pastors and teachers"* (Ephesians 4:11), for the purpose of *"equipping…the saints for the work of ministry, for the edifying of the body of Christ"* (verse 12). The church has need of these individuals *"till we all come to the unity of the faith and of the knowledge of the Son of God, to a perfect man, to the measure of the stature of the fullness of Christ"* (verse 13)—none of which has happened yet.

The reason we still need the fivefold offices to actively exist is laid out in verses 14–15:

> *…that we should no longer be children, tossed to and fro and carried about with every wind of doctrine, by the trickery of men, in the cunning craftiness of deceitful plotting, but, speaking the truth in love, [that we] may grow up in all things into Him who is the head—Christ.*

When we fulfill our God-given roles, we help the rest of the church to grow in its walk and relationship with the Lord, because *"the **whole body**, joined and knit together by what **every** joint supplies, according to the effective working by which **every** part does its share, causes growth of the body for the edifying of itself in love"* (Ephesians 4:16).

Every person in the church is necessary. (See 1 Corinthians 12:12; Romans 12:4.) When each person advances, everyone else is encouraged to step up to the plate. The Word tells us that even those who seem to be the least in the kingdom are actually the most necessary. (See 1 Corinthians 12:22.)

The Church's Job

Many pastors get frustrated because their congregations refuse to advance. It is often difficult to get people to step out and operate in what they have been taught.

Having faith means believing God enough to do what He says you can do. As James put it, *"Someone will say, 'You have faith, and I have works.'*

Show me your faith without your works, and I will show you my faith by my works" (James 2:18).

Title Wave

Years ago, the Lord told me, "There's about to be a 'title wave' in the church. Don't get caught up in it." Sure enough, there was a flood of individuals demanding to be called 'apostle' or 'prophet.' I've known many true apostles and prophets, and *none* of them demanded a title. In fact, many did not want a title at all.

Worth noting here is that, within the pages of this book, I refer to my spiritual papa, Bob Jones, as Prophet Bob Jones. I do so as a means of proper identification, because there is a Bob Jones of Bob Jones University, and that is not the Bob Jones I'm referring to. But, to be sure, Prophet Bob Jones never required a title.

Let's return to our previous discussion, and look at a brief description of the fivefold ministry.

Apostles

For many years, a false spirit of apostleship has occurred by which self-designated, so-called apostles come in, take over, and run the show, beating others up with their religious spirit, and demanding subservience and titles. They then extract large offerings, only to leave the churches they have "served" in a shambles, riddled with divisions. That's not a biblical example of true apostleship.

As we examine the Word, we see that apostles are to be the mothers and fathers of the fivefold ministry. They discern where others fit, and assist them in becoming equipped and activated in their God-ordained calls.

In Acts 18:24–28, we have an exemplification of the real deal in the apostles Priscilla and Aquila, who met and ministered to Apollos. Hearing Apollos teach, they recognized him as being eloquent and learned in the Scriptures. However, they also noticed that he spoke about the future coming of a Messiah, rather than acknowledging that the Messiah had already come. Not wanting to embarrass him, they did not correct him in public but instead tracked him down in private and encouraged him. They blessed his ability to teach, and lovingly informed him of the life, death, and resurrection of Jesus. Their visit inspired Apollos to share the Good News, bringing many to Christ.

Like natural parents in relation to their children, true apostolic parents hold a higher level of authority among the fivefold offices and within the church. They are also likely to operate in signs and wonders. Their authority comes from their having been appointed by God (rather than by themselves), from the relationships they build, from their proven track record of integrity, and from many years of knowledge and experience. It isn't sufficient to simply designate oneself as an apostle.

Today, a number of self-appointed apostles offer unsatisfying support for their spiritual children, and they charge a monthly or yearly fee, plus a large honorarium, on top of other unnecessary expenses that may include first-class travel and lavish accommodations.

These individuals in no way resemble the apostles of the Bible, of whom Jesus said, *"I know your works, your labor, your patience, and that you cannot bear those who are evil. And you have tested those who say they are apostles and are not, and have found them liars"* (Revelation 2:2).

The apostles whose lives are recorded in the New Testament displayed the love of God and developed *relationships* with those they served, maintaining communication even when they were on the road. They spent quality time with their constituents and spoke the truth in love. They were devoted to the Word and to prayer, travailing over those in their care. They counseled, ministered, prayed, healed, and operated in deliverance, signs, wonders, and miracles. They helped congregations moderate various issues that arose among their members. And they assisted in starting new works as they traveled, trusting God to provide for their needs as they went. (See Matthew 10:9–10; Luke 9:3–5.)

Some people like to describe the fivefold ministry by using the fingers of one hand to illustrate the different offices. The thumb is used to designate the apostolic ministry, but not to indicate that apostles put people "under their thumb" in order to control them. Rather, because the thumb is under each of the other fingers, it represents the undergirding aspect of the apostolic to the other offices.

Prophets

Some people view prophets as mean-spirited individuals. Any true man or woman of God must be marked by a spirit of love. The attitude of prophets should be that of the apostle Paul when he wrote, *"Though I have the gift of prophecy, and understand all mysteries and all knowledge, and though I have all faith, so that I could remove mountains, but have not love, I am nothing"* (1 Corinthians 13:2)

The fruit of the Holy Spirit, as listed in the book of Galatians, should be evident in the life of every Christian, especially in Christian leaders: *"love, joy, peace, longsuffering, kindness, goodness, faithfulness, gentleness, self-control"* (Galatians 5:22–23).

If Someone Prophesies, Does That Make Him or Her a Prophet?

All may prophesy, according to 1 Corinthians 14:31; but that doesn't mean that every prophetic utterance is made by someone who is a prophet. Remember, in the Bible, even a donkey prophesied. (See Numbers 22:21–39.)

TRUE PROPHETS HAVE EARNED THEIR OFFICE
THROUGH MANY YEARS OF PROVEN SERVICE.
THEY DON'T FLAUNT THE TITLE OF PROPHET.
THE HOLY SPIRIT WILL PROVE THEM, AND
OTHERS WILL ACKNOWLEDGE IT.

Three areas of revelatory authority include:

(1) The *office* of the prophet. (See Ephesians 4:11.)

True prophets have earned their office through many years of proven service. They don't flaunt the title of prophet. The Holy Spirit will prove them, and others will acknowledge it. They may be able to tell you what you have dreamed and then interpret the dream, as well as receive names, phone numbers, and other details in supernatural ways—an ability lacking in people who are merely prophetically gifted.

(2) The *gift* of prophecy. (See 1 Corinthians 12:10.)

The gift of prophecy is just that—a gift. If someone doesn't have that particular gift, he or she can ask the Lord for it, and He will grant it as He sees fit. (See Matthew 7:7–11.)

(3) The *spirit* of prophecy. (See, for example, 1 Samuel 10:10–11.)

When the spirit of prophecy comes upon a group of people, whoever opens their mouth as a willing vessel may be used.

If you operate on a prophetic team, you will notice how the spirit of prophecy will hover over your team, and each team member may tap into it. Greater "unction to function" occurs as the spirit of prophecy jumps from one to another.

God *speaks* to us all. He promises that He will pour out His Spirit upon *all* flesh, and that *all* will prophesy. (See Joel 2:28–29; Acts 2:17–18.)

The Heart of a Prophet

Being a prophet isn't a status symbol. God often refers to prophets as His servants. (See, for example, 2 Kings 9:7; 17:13; Jeremiah 7:25; 26:5; 29:19; 35:15; 44:4; Ezekiel 38:17; Zechariah 1:6.) Being a prophet carries great responsibility and requires the qualities of love and compassion, as well as the act of intercession for God's people. (See, for example, Jeremiah 27:18.)

God is love. (See 1 John 4:8, 16.) If a prophet has been sent by God to warn people of His judgment, that prophet should desire that his or her listeners repent in order to avoid punishment. He or she should *not* be disappointed when the people listen and repent, as Jonah was when God sent him to the Ninevites and the people avoided the wrath of God. (See Jonah 4:1.)

God's promise in 2 Chronicles 7:14 applies to everyone:

If my people who are called by My name will humble themselves, and pray and seek My face, and turn from their wicked ways, then I will hear from heaven, and will forgive their sin and heal their land.

We don't prophesy warnings to be right. We issue warnings to call people to repentance, so that God might relent and lift the judgment.

Evangelists

Evangelists aren't the only ones equipped to usher people into the kingdom of God. In 2 Timothy 4:5, Paul encourages everyone to do the work of an evangelist. And as it says in Proverbs 11:30, *"He who wins souls is wise."*

Jesus began to teach and to operate in evangelism as soon as He came out of the desert after being tempted by Satan. (See Matthew 4:17–22.)

While it is true that the primary purpose of the office of an evangelist is bringing souls into the kingdom, evangelists may also operate in other areas of gifting, including healing, prophecy, and so forth.

The Bible says that no one comes to Jesus unless the Father calls him or her. (See John 6:44.) In many cases, there is an appointed time when an individual is most likely to finally give his or her life to the Lord. It may be that we are called to plant seeds that someone else will later harvest. (See 1 Corinthians 3:7.) Thus, we should try to do only what the Father says do if we want to have a fruitful evangelistic ministry. That's what Jesus did, after all. (See John 5:19.)

We should also avoid pressuring others to believe, because this technique usually backfires. Standing on a street corner, thumping a Bible with one's fist, and shouting at people that they are going to hell isn't very inviting, is it? The truth is, people who are on their way to hell usually know it already, and don't need someone to tell them. What they need to hear instead is this: "If you know you're on your way to hell, I have good news— there's a way out!"

Prophetic evangelism entails seeking God for a word for someone that will change his or her life and bring that person into the kingdom. Prophetic evangelism is what Jesus practiced with the woman at the well in

John 4:1–26. It was also practiced by the prophet Ananias with Saul before he became the apostle Paul. (See Acts 9:1–19.)

PROPHETIC EVANGELISM ENTAILS SEEKING GOD FOR A WORD FOR SOMEONE THAT WILL CHANGE HIS OR HER LIFE AND BRING THAT PERSON INTO THE KINGDOM.

The only things we can take with us when we leave this world are the souls of those we have brought into the kingdom of God. What an honor and joy it will be for us to be able to say, "Look who all I brought with me!" on that final day.

Pastors

The title of pastor usually refers to someone who heads up a church. When we talk about pastors, we often refer to them as shepherds, and to their congregations as their sheep. There's a good reason for that, and it originates in the Bible.

Sheep are followers. Shepherds are leaders who carefully tend the sheep so they will head in the right direction. They feed and water the sheep, trim their wool when needed, dress any wounds, and protect them from wolves.

The Lord is depicted in various places as a shepherd, perhaps most notably in Psalm 23. Consider this excerpt:

The LORD is my shepherd; I shall not want. He makes me to lie down in green pastures; He leads me beside the still waters. He restores my soul; He leads me in the paths of righteousness for His name's sake.

(Psalm 23:1–3)

Jesus says of Himself, *"I am the good shepherd. The good shepherd gives His life for the sheep"* (John 10:11).

A shepherd is a spiritual parent who lays down his or her life to raise God's children of all ages, with all their baggage.

We find the following exhortation to pastors in 1 Peter 5:2–4:

Shepherd the flock of God which is among you, serving as overseers, not by compulsion but willingly, not for dishonest gain but eagerly; nor as being lords over those entrusted to you, but being examples to the flock; and when the Chief Shepherd [Jesus] appears, you will receive the crown of glory that does not fade away.

God's heart is to provide *loving* shepherds. He says to the sheep in Jeremiah 3:15, *"I will give you shepherds according to My heart, who will feed you with knowledge and understanding."*

When God sees shepherds who are neglectful and abusive, His heart is wrenched. To them, He says:

The weak you have not strengthened, nor have you healed those who were sick, nor bound up the broken, nor brought back what was driven away, nor sought what was lost; but with force and cruelty you have ruled them. So they were scattered because there was no shepherd; and they became food for all the beasts of the field when they were scat-tered.   (Ezekiel 34:4–5)

In Revelation 7:17, Jesus promises, *"The Lamb who is in the midst of the throne will shepherd them and lead them to living fountains of waters. And God will wipe away every tear from their eyes."*

Teachers

Teachers love research and learning, as well imparting to others what they have discovered. They take seriously the directive to *"be diligent to present yourself approved to God, a worker who does not need to be ashamed, rightly dividing the word of truth"* (2 Timothy 2:15).

During His earthly life, Jesus was the ultimate teacher. He loved to gather people together and teach them for hours at a time. Those who have the gift of teaching are like that—they tirelessly enjoy sharing the knowledge and wisdom they have gained through their studies and experiences.

Scripture tells us we should all be teachers of what we have learned. (See Hebrews 5:12.) In this way, we are like living water. The difference between stagnant water and living water is that living water not only has a place of entrance but also an exit, so that it cleanses and renews the streams where it flows. Stagnant water just sits there, becoming lifeless, putrid, and stale. We become the same when we stifle what we have learned rather than sharing it with others.

Anointed teachers bring life and clarity to that which they teach. They impart knowledge in such a practical way that anyone can understand it, becoming changed and enriched in the process. Anointed teachers are often gifted storytellers who grip the attention of their students and ignite passion for the topic being discussed. They are some of the best authors, painting pictures with their words.

Perhaps the strictest biblical warning issued to the office of teacher is found in James 3:1: *"My brethren, let not many of you become teachers, knowing that we shall receive a stricter judgment."*

Those who stand in the teaching office must make sure that what they study is scripturally sound. God's Word should be established as the plumb line for all that we reference. Never would we want to impart heresy to anyone. A warning along these lines may be found in 2 Peter 2:1–3.

The Ongoing Importance of the Fivefold Ministry

The offices of the fivefold ministry are still vital in the church, and will remain so until Jesus returns. Some individuals have abused these offices, unfortunately; but thanks be to God that we have many people who are faithful in fulfilling these roles. We need them, and they need us. No one can answer his or her call without assistance. Let's treasure and support one another in what we have been called to do.

We need a fully operational fivefold ministry in the church today. Like the five smooth stones David had on hand when he hurled the stone that felled the giant Goliath, those who are sent out by God to fill the roles of the fivefold ministries will expose the giant lies of the enemy—the lies that say the church no longer has power—and will cause them to crumble.

PRAYER

Dear Lord, thank You that Your power is still available for us to operate in today. Give us hearing ears, discerning spirits, and teachable, compassionate hearts. May none of us pass through this earth without walking in the fullness of our calling. In Jesus's name, amen.

2

THE PURPOSE OF PROPHECY

Venturing into unfamiliar spiritual areas can prove a bit scary. When I began my prophetic journey, I feared doing something wrong. I wanted the words I gave to others to be scripturally sound, so I delved into the Word to make sure that the Bible supported the idea of prophesying in this day and age. My searching confirmed that God's heart *is* that we would use the gifts He gives to us, including the gift of prophecy. Additionally, because God is not a respecter of persons (see Acts 10:34 KJV), He will use any willing vessel. (See Joel 2:28–29; Acts 2:17–18.)

The Bible tells us that God wants us to *"earnestly desire"* His gifts (1 Corinthians 12:31; see also 1 Corinthians 14:6, 12). He wants us to be zealous about the gifts He has for us, desiring to use them in order to have a positive effect on the lives of others. It's not altogether unlike the way we feel when we give someone else a gift: We hope that we have given something the recipient will be pleased with and will want to use often.

In order to be good stewards of God's gifts, we must exercise and use those gifts properly.

As each one has received a gift, minister it to one another as good stewards of the manifold grace of God. If anyone speaks, let him speak as the oracles of God. If anyone ministers, let him do it with the ability which God supplies, that in all things God may be glorified through Jesus Christ, to whom belong the glory and the dominion forever and ever. Amen. (1 Peter 4:10–11)

Having then gifts differing according to the grace that is given to us, let us use them: if prophecy, let us prophesy in proportion to our faith.

(Romans 12:6)

Why Should We Prophesy?

Prophecy is simply hearing from God and relaying to others what He has said. And why would we want to convey what He has said?

1. We Prophesy So That We May Obey God

Deuteronomy 29:29 says, "*The secret things belong to the LORD our God, but those things which are revealed belong to us and to our children forever, that we may do all the words of this law.*" In other words, God wants us to know what is on His heart so that He can help us to be obedient and thereby obtain the blessings that He has for us.

All believers have the ability to hear from God for themselves; we should never default to seeking to hear from Him through someone else, for that practice borders on the illicit art of divination. We are called to seek God and His instructions, not the instructions of other people. Any person who tries to make others dependent upon him or her to hear from God is operating in a spirit of witchcraft.

The fact of the matter is, some people tend to grow accustomed to calling on someone else to give them a word from God rather than seeking God on their own. That's why I prefer not to prophesy to people when they call me on the phone, asking for a word. I prefer to teach people how to hear God for themselves.

SOME PEOPLE TEND TO GROW ACCUSTOMED
TO CALLING ON SOMEONE ELSE TO GIVE THEM
A WORD FROM GOD RATHER THAN SEEKING
GOD ON THEIR OWN.

On the other hand, if we are under attack, we sometimes become so confounded that we can't seem to hear from God for ourselves when we are seeking confirmation in order to avoid doing the wrong thing. No one wants to get into a situation that would constitute a detour from God's plans. However, when detours happen, God may well send someone to speak into our lives—someone He will use to deliver a word of direction to get us back on track and to keep us there. Sometimes, we may be the one He has sent to deliver such a word to someone else.

2. We Prophesy to Encourage Others

Once again, God is love (see 1 John 4:8, 16), and He desires to express love and encouragement to His creation. Many wounded people don't feel loved. An encouraging prophetic word could very well save someone's life by, say, preventing him or her from committing suicide. God is faithful to send prophetic words to pull people out of the enemy's lies and into an abundant life in Jesus.

God also desires to provide us with correction and warnings when those are called for. I will cover these types of prophetic words in greater detail in a later chapter. For now, let me explain the encouragement aspect of the prophetic.

The apostle Paul talks a lot about the process of encouragement in his first letter to the church at Corinth.

> He who prophesies speaks edification and exhortation and comfort to men. (1 Corinthians 14:3)

> He who prophesies edifies the church. (1 Corinthians 14:4)

> I wish you all spoke with tongues, but even more that you prophesied; for he who prophesies is greater than he who speaks with tongues, unless indeed he interprets, that the church may receive edification. (1 Corinthians 14:5)

> Since you are zealous for spiritual gifts, let it be for the edification of the church that you seek to excel. (1 Corinthians 14:12)

Let all things be done for edification.   (1 Corinthians 14:26)

Let's turn to *Merriam-Webster's Dictionary* as we discuss what it means to encourage or edify someone.

One meaning of the prefix of the word *encourage,* "en-," is "put into or onto." *Courage* means "mental or moral strength to venture, persevere, and withstand danger, fear, or difficulty." To *edify* means "to instruct and improve especially in moral and religious knowledge: uplift."

So, what ought to happen when we give someone a prophetic word from the Lord? They should be built up and filled with the courage and strength to persevere and to withstand danger, fear, or difficulty.

It is awesome for us to be used by God to infuse others with courage. As it says in Amos 3:8, *"A lion has roared! Who will not fear? The LORD God has spoken! Who can but prophesy?"*

There have been many times when I was feeling low and God used a prophetic word to encourage me, letting me know that He still sees me, loves me, and has good plans for me. And He has used me to deliver a similar message to others.

MOST PEOPLE WHO ARE IN NEED OF
CORRECTION ARE ALREADY AWARE OF IT;
WHAT THEY NEED TO KNOW IS THE GOOD
NEWS OF HOW TO GET OUT OF THE SITUATION
THAT HAS THEM ENTRAPPED.

Some people think they are called to be one of God's designated "sledgehammers," constantly bringing correction and messages of gloom and doom to others. As I've said before, most people who are in need of correction are already aware of it; what they need to know is the good news of how to get out of the situation that has them entrapped.

Often, a prophetic word is simply a word of encouragement rather than a futuristic pronouncement—a statement that will motivate someone in the midst of an intense battle to press on to victory.

There are times when messages of correction and conviction are in order. But, in most cases, it is the people who feel "called" to correct others who are really in need of correction. They walk around with a proverbial chip on their shoulder, doing a great deal of damage in the process.

As we have seen, God's Word says that prophecy is for the purpose of encouragement. Yet some people choose to operate in a spirit of charismatic witchcraft in an effort to control others. They presume to chasten other people for "not obeying the Lord" if those people do not "obey" the so-called prophetic word they have been given. In reality, they are voicing their own opinions and controlling directives. We must watch out for this Jezebel-like spirit, which we will discuss further in chapter 18.

Many prophetic ministries have wisely chosen to adopt sets of guidelines such as this: "If a person isn't in your area of responsibility, he or she is not in your area of authority for correction. Therefore, take any words of correction to the leadership, and let them judge." Anyone who believes he or she has received a prophetic word of correction is required to write down that word and submit it to the ministry leadership to handle. In addition, he or she may be called in for questioning or help in delivering the word in the presence of the leadership. You might be surprised by how much the practice of such "notes of accountability" cuts down on the number of such incidents. Those who want to bring the correction often get mad and then accuse the leaders of abusing control for expecting them to face the person they are accusing.

3. We Prophesy to Bring Others to Christ

If all prophesy, and an unbeliever or an uninformed person comes in, he is convinced by all, he is convicted by all. And thus the secrets of his heart are revealed; and so, falling down on his face, he will worship God and report that God is truly among you. (1 Corinthians 14:24–25)

Like Jesus did, we may be used by God to prophesy to someone in order to lead him or her to salvation. This practice is referred to as "prophetic evangelism." Jesus demonstrated prophetic evangelism in His interactions with the woman at the well (see John 4:1–26) and with the woman caught in adultery (see John 8:1–11).

Prophecy has the power to change people completely. (See 1 Samuel 10:6.) We find a vivid example of this truth in the conversion of Saul, who became the apostle Paul, recounted by Paul himself in Acts 26:14–18:

> *I heard a voice speaking to me and saying in the Hebrew language, "Saul, Saul, why are you persecuting Me? It is hard for you to kick against the goads." So I said, "Who are You, Lord?" And He said, "I am Jesus, whom you are persecuting. But rise and stand on your feet; for I have appeared to you for this purpose, to make you a minister and a witness both of the things which you have seen and of the things which I will yet reveal to you. I will deliver you from the Jewish people, as well as from the Gentiles, to whom I now send you, to open their eyes, in order to turn them from darkness to light, and from the power of Satan to God, that they may receive forgiveness of sins and an inheritance among those who are sanctified by faith in Me."*

How powerful it is to realize that we can help to turn souls from the power of Satan to God. It's exciting that the Lord would allow us to take part in such an incredible adventure!

The church is in the time period of going out into the highways and byways, and compelling the harvest to come in. (See Luke 14:23.) The great revival that many are prophesying will not happen *inside* the church. Most people in there are already saved. Trying to get people inside the church to save them is like fishing inside of a boat. It's time to cast our nets on the other side—out into the world. There, we will bring in the "big haul." The big harvest that many have seen with their spiritual eyes is yet to come.

The marketplace is where the majority of today's great harvest will take place. It is where we live, eat, work, shop, and play. God has positioned you in the airplane seat next to that businessperson for a reason. He has that server assigned to your table at a restaurant so that he or she will hear His heart and His plans for him or her. He has that person in line behind you at the grocery store today to hear a word of encouragement.

Who May Prophesy?

The manifestation of the Spirit is given to each one for the profit of all.
(1 Corinthians 12:7)

You can all prophesy one by one, that all may learn and all may be encouraged. (1 Corinthians 14:31)

Do you think God really means *"all"*? I sure do.

The Old Testament prophesies the following, which is echoed in the New Testament:

And it shall come to pass afterward that I will pour out My Spirit upon all flesh; your sons and your daughters shall prophesy, your old men shall dream dreams, your young men shall see visions. And also on my menservants and on My maidservants I will pour out My Spirit in those days. (Joel 2:28–29; see also Acts 2:17–18)

That pretty much covers every person of every age. Remember, God is no respecter of persons. He pours out His Spirit out upon *all* flesh, *all* ages. You are no exception. If we don't praise Him, the rocks will cry out. (See Luke 19:40.) If we don't prophesy, He may speak through animals instead. (See Numbers 22.)

GOD IS NO RESPECTER OF PERSONS. HE POURS OUT HIS SPIRIT OUT UPON *ALL* FLESH, *ALL* AGES. YOU ARE NO EXCEPTION.

No one is forcing you to do prophesy, not even Jesus. If the enemy of your soul has told you that you can't do it, he is a liar. You *do* hear God's voice. You can be as much a part of this adventure as you allow yourself to be.

One time, when I held back from giving a word to someone, the Lord clearly spoke to me. He said, "Give that word to them. It doesn't belong to you. I gave it to you to give to them. Now give it to who it belongs to."

As God's ambassador, you have come into this world for such a time as this. Embrace who you are, and enjoy doing what God says you can do. Infuse someone else with courage today.

PRAYER

Lord, please help us to get past all the lies of the enemy. May we allow ourselves to be effectively used by You to infuse Your people with courage. We will give to You all the glory for anything good that's done. In Jesus's name, amen.

3

BASICS OF PERSONAL PROPHECY

Merriam-Webster defines *prophecy* as "an inspired utterance of a prophet; the function or vocation of a prophet; specifically: the inspired declaration of divine will and purpose; a prediction of something to come."[1]

Jesus says, "*My sheep hear My voice, and I know them, and they follow Me*" (John 10:27).

God gives *every* believer the ability to hear His voice. (See Acts 2:17–18.) In this chapter, we will discuss what the Bible says about personal prophecy, how to attune your spirit to hear from God, and how to teach and activate others in the skill of personal prophecy.

A personal prophetic word should never be given greater authority than the Scriptures, and we should also test every prophecy according to the Scriptures. Moreover, we should not follow the advice of anyone who tells us something that awakens a sense of uneasiness in our spirit.

Where Does Prophecy Come From?

Revelation 19:10 says, "*The testimony of Jesus is the spirit of prophecy.*" Earlier on in the book of Revelation, it tells us that Satan is defeated by the blood of the Lamb and the word of our testimony. (See Revelation 12:11.)

Often, a prophetic word is our testimony spoken to us in advance. When we go through trials, we may receive encouragement from a word

---

1. "Prophecy." Merriam-Webster.com. https://www.merriam-webster.com/dictionary/prophecy (accessed July 31,2018).

that assures us of eventual victory. We can use that word to wage war in prayer and to advance toward the fulfillment of that promise. We might pray something like this: "Right now, I proclaim that the situation I am in will not prevail. Through His prophetic word, God has promised _____ [state the promise here]. In Jesus's name, I cancel all assignments that are contrary to His promise."

We will engage in spiritual warfare in our process of advancing the kingdom. Thankfully, God gives us prophetic words to help us battle more effectively.

Prophecy Is a Gift of the Holy Spirit

The nine gifts of the Spirit are listed in the twelfth chapter of 1 Corinthians:

> *To one is given the word of wisdom through the Spirit* [the understanding and application of prophetic knowledge or insight], *to another the word of knowledge* [the spiritual revelation of information that is not knowable in the natural] *through the same Spirit, to another faith by the same Spirit, to another gifts of healings by the same Spirit, to another the working of miracles, to another prophecy, to another discerning of spirits, to another different kinds of tongues, to another the interpretation of tongues. But one and the same Spirit works all these things, distributing to each one individually as He wills.*   (1 Corinthians 12:8–11)

Each of the gifts also may be used in conjunction with one or more of the other gifts. For instance, the Lord may give a revealing prophetic word of knowledge about someone's health to help bring about healing. In another situation, someone may prophesy in tongues *and* receive the interpretation of that prophecy.

Jesus is the only mediator between God and man. (See 1 Timothy 2:5.) We should never become totally dependent on another person to consistently hear from God for us. God is the giver of gifts, and He is the One upon whom we should depend. To do otherwise is to disrespect His gifts and to treat them as divination.

God's words convey His heart and plans. Speaking through the prophet Jeremiah, He says, *"For I know the plans I have for you… plans to prosper you and not to harm you, plans to give you hope and a future"* (Jeremiah 29:11 NIV).

WE SHOULD NEVER BECOME TOTALLY DEPENDENT ON ANOTHER PERSON TO CONSISTENTLY HEAR FROM GOD FOR US. GOD IS THE GIVER OF GIFTS, AND HE IS THE ONE UPON WHOM WE SHOULD DEPEND.

God speaks prophetically by His Spirit to our spiritual hearts and minds. Often, this happens when your mind entertains a thought that you *know* isn't your own. Prophecy is a *spiritual* knowledge regarding something about which you have no *natural* knowledge.

"Oath-Level Prophetic Words" Versus "Personal Prophetic Words"

The only *oath-level* prophetic words are those found in the Bible. Merriam-Webster defines *oath* as "a solemn attestation of the truth or inviolability of one's words; something (such as a promise) corroborated by an oath."[2] When God Himself has attested to something, it *will* happen. For example, He promised the coming of a Messiah, and it occurred. Now there is the promise of the return of Jesus. Whether anyone believes it or tries to stop it is irrelevant. It *will* occur.

Personal prophetic words often carry contingencies. The recipients of personal prophetic words must deal with:

---

2. "Oath." Merriam-Webster.com. https://www.merriam-webster,com/dictionary/oath (accessed July 31, 2018).

- their ability to interpret what they are hearing.

- their own personal will.

- timing.

- knowing and walking out anything they need to do to accomplish what the word has prescribed.

- the will and actions of others involved.

- the ability of the person giving the word to hear it correctly and convey it with adequate clarity.

We find a useful example in the words of Mordecai to his cousin Esther as he encouraged her to act on behalf of the Jewish people:

> *If you remain completely silent at this time, relief and deliverance will arise for the Jews from another place, but you and your father's house will perish. Yet who knows whether you have come to the kingdom for such a time as this?* (Esther 4:14)

Mordecai didn't say, "Esther, you are the only one who can save the Jews. If you don't act, all our people will perish." Rather, he said, "Who knows whether you've been called for such a time as this?" Furthermore, "If you decide not to act, someone else will step up to the plate." Had Esther chosen to disregard her cousin's word, there would have been consequences.

We see that Esther had a choice of whether to accept and act on the prophetic word or to ignore it. God didn't force her to do anything. In the same way, it is not up to us to control what others do with the prophetic words we give them.

God Speaks in Various Ways

God speaks in a variety of ways. Sometimes, He speaks through His written Word and reveals a specific Bible verse to give to someone. Sometimes, He gives us a vision—a mental image or a scene—that we are to convey. Sometimes, what we receive comes as a thought or a still, small voice in our head. (See 1 Kings 19:12.)

God does not always communicate with us via a prophetic word spoken by someone. He may speak through a movie, a song, a billboard, or a simple statement we overhear someone saying. In any case, the word will be so strong that it will stick with us, giving us a sense of *knowing* in our spirit that God is speaking to us.

God isn't just Someone we worship in church. He's the God who meets us in the midst of our dark nights of the soul, in times when we are all alone, lying facedown on the carpet. He's the God who is with us in the middle of a traffic accident, as we cry out while our vehicle is being hurled across a busy highway. He's the God who hears us cry out as an assailant comes at us with a knife or a gun in a dark alley. He's the God who soars high above the clouds with us as the airplane we're traveling in takes a sudden dive. He's the God who wraps His arms around us and whispers words of comfort in our ear as we sit at the bedside of a loved one who is slowly slipping into eternity.

GOD DOES NOT ALWAYS COMMUNICATE WITH US VIA A PROPHETIC WORD SPOKEN BY SOMEONE. HE MAY SPEAK THROUGH A MOVIE, A SONG, A BILLBOARD, OR A SIMPLE STATEMENT WE OVERHEAR SOMEONE SAYING.

He not only hears us cry out at such times, but He also speaks words of comfort as He wraps us in His love.

Do Not Be Discouraged If You Do Not Receive a Public Word

A visiting prophet doesn't necessarily need to single us out and give us a personal word. Sometimes, the word we need to hear comes to us within the text of a teaching. It will be so full of prophetic nuggets that we feel the teaching was intended specifically for us.

God can speak to us directly; we may hear Him for ourselves. Or, He may use an ordinary person to deliver a prophetic message to us. There may even be times when we have received enough prophetic words to pursue that He chooses to remain silent, because He doesn't want to give us additional instructions until we have followed the instructions we have already received.

Don't leave a meeting saying you didn't receive anything. You get what you believe you have received. God says to us, *"According to your faith let it be to you"* (Matthew 9:29).

The promises God gave to Abraham are for all who will receive them, as are the words we hear others receive. Just say to the Lord, "I receive that, too!"

I was a part of MorningStar Ministries, one of the top prophetic ministries in the world, from its inception. However, for the longest time, I *never* received a word. I would show up at church and at School of the Spirit meetings before anyone else and get a front-row seat. The major prophets of our day would come and prophesy over everyone sitting in front of me, behind me, and on either side of me, but never to me.

After a while, I became a little paranoid, and more than a little overdramatic. I thought to myself, *Prophecy is for telling our futures. I'm not getting a word, so maybe that means I'm going to die.*

I attended a big conference organized by the ministry, and there was a "prophetic mall" at the end of one service. Participating ministers went to different areas of the building, and we were told to choose a line to stand in to receive a word. I tried every line. Every time it came to my turn, the leader walked away. I thought, *Am I dead already and don't know it?*

Then a man walked up to me and said, "Can I talk to you for a minute?"

I was shocked. "You mean, you see me?" I asked him.

"Uh, yes," he replied, with a look of confusion. "I was watching and saw that every time you were the next one to be ministered to, the person walked away. I felt bad for you. So, I asked God what the deal was."

"Did He tell you?" I asked, amazed.

"Yes. He said to tell you that you already hear clearly for yourself. In fact, one day, people will be lined up to hear from God through you. So, He wanted you to know how it feels to be the one in the room who felt like she needed ministering to the most, but didn't get a word. That way, you'll look for that person when it's your turn to minister."

What a powerful explanation that was. I can't say I believed what the man said at the time, but his word has come to pass. To this day, I always look for the one who needs encouraging the most.

What Type of Person Will God Use to Prophesy?

Those who are the least likely to succeed become those most likely to succeed when God enters the picture. He then receives the glory He deserves.

Multiple authors are quoted as having said, "God doesn't call the qualified; He qualifies the called." God is "loser friendly." The greater our afflictions or failures, the more miraculously God can use us.

THOSE WHO ARE THE LEAST LIKELY TO SUCCEED BECOME THOSE MOST LIKELY TO SUCCEED WHEN GOD ENTERS THE PICTURE. HE THEN RECEIVES THE GLORY HE DESERVES.

In God's economy, the "least likely to succeed" become the *most* likely to succeed. Why? Because, in our weakness, God is strong. (See 2 Corinthians 12:9–10.) There is nothing that's impossible for Him. (See, for example, Matthew 19:26.)

Often, when men and women first step out into ministry, one of their children begins to go astray. In these cases, one of the best things that parents can do is continue to pursue their purpose, no matter what, thereby setting an example for their children that nothing can cause them to quit. God never quits just because some of His kids are out of order, does He?

While the world often disqualifies people, God forgives, accepts, and uses the testimonies of many who have failed.

The word *testimony* means "a formal written or spoken statement...; evidence or proof of something; a public recounting of a religious conversion or experience."[3] God has saved many people from addictions to drugs and alcohol, prostitution, drug trafficking, abuse, robbery, murder, and more. Their testimonies have great power.

Rick Joyner has said, "In the very areas where you have been wounded, once healed, you then have the authority to heal others."

The Bible says that Satan is defeated by the blood of the Lamb and the word of our testimony. (See Revelation 12:11.) Speaking our testimony aloud destroys the work of the enemy in others' lives, as well as in our own. The key is not allowing the enemy to blackmail us. Our testimony can become our most powerful weapon for subduing and defeating the enemy, in our own lives as well as in the lives of others.

The Least Likely to Succeed

The condemning voices of the enemy try to discourage God's people from fulfilling their calling. When God called Gideon, Gideon argued that he was not qualified because he came from the poorest clan in his region, and was the poorest one in all of his clan. (See Judges 6:15.) He soon realized that he would have to trust in God more than in his own abilities to accomplish the tasks ahead of him.

God knows what He has placed within each of us. Even if we do not believe in ourselves, we can trust that the God who made us knows what we are capable of.

One of the most unlikely heroes in the Bible is the apostle Paul. He started out as a devout Jew who murdered Christians. It must have been

3. https://en.oxforddictionaries.com/definition/testimony (accessed June 8, 2018).

scary for believers to trust him when he converted to Christianity and started ministering to Christians, instead. I'm sure some feared he may have pretended in order to get inside their group to kill them, too. But He is a true Bible hero.

Women

There are many women who are afraid to step out in ministry. Yet a host of women have succeeded in this realm. In the Bible, the prophetess Deborah became one of the judges of Israel. (See Judges 4:4–5.) More recently, God has mightily used such women as Kathryn Kuhlman, Aimee Semple McPherson, Maria Woodworth-Etter, and Mother Teresa to spread His name and advance His kingdom on the earth. And there are many women involved in ministry today, some of whom have experienced hardships, such as divorce, that others might point out in order to disqualify them from their work. But, as one man once pointed out to me, if divorce is grounds for disqualification from ministry, then God would be disqualified, because He divorced Israel. (See Jeremiah 3:8.)

Children

Every so often, our church has prophetic teams that are made up of children. You'd be surprised at what has come forth from the work of these teams. It is the same Holy Spirit inside all believers. He is not restricted by the age of those through whom He works.

During a time when I had—unwisely—been spending too much time on the road, to the detriment of my health, I was humbled when God used a child to speak wisdom to me. A young boy came to me and said, "God said to tell you that you need to take a break off the road for a while so you can rest up and not get sick. Here's some money to help you do that." He then handed me the money he had received for his birthday. How sweet! I tried to tell him I didn't want to take his money, but his mother said that doing so would crush his heart, so I accepted the money and gave the boy a big hug.

> Out of the mouths of babes and nursing infants You have ordained strength, because of Your enemies, that you may silence the enemy and the avenger. (Psalm 8:2)

Ministering Angels

The Lord sometimes uses angelic messengers to deliver a word in due season. He did so in the book of Revelation, which records an angel's messages to various churches. We read, *"I, Jesus, have sent My angel to testify to you…in the churches"* (Revelation 22:16).

Hebrews 1:14 asks, *"Are they* [angels] *not all ministering spirits sent forth to minister for those who will inherit salvation?"*

I often travel throughout the country to minister prophetically to people. One time, I heard words in my spirit, but they came so rapidly that I couldn't relay them fast enough. I realized that it must have been a ministering angel speaking to me. I had to stop and whisper, "Please, slower! I can't keep up!" The message then slowed down enough that I could understand what was being said and could also convey it.

After the service, not knowing what I had experienced, several people told me they had seen angels standing beside me as I spoke.

Prisoners

I have ministered with various groups in several prisons. A prison of male inmates in Alabama had been experiencing revival, and I was called in to teach and activate the men in prophetic ministry. They were very receptive, and the ministry team and I had a great time. Even so, I wondered how our ministry would pan out. Who would those men minister to in such a setting? Many of them were serving life sentences.

A couple of months later, I received an amazing report that made me weep. It involved a man in his eighties who had ministered at the prison for many years. After his wife died, he wasn't the same. He told the men at the prison that he had decided to retire. The inmates were sad to see him go, and with the help of the guards, they planned a surprise party for his final visit to the prison. They even baked him a cake in the prison kitchen. At the end of the party, the prisoners asked the man if they could pray for him before he left. He agreed, and they prayed for him, then began to give him prophetic words.

The Holy Spirit showed up that day. It turns out that the elderly minister had been planning to go home and commit suicide after the meeting that day. But because of the prophetic words the men gave to him through the revelation of the Lord, the man was delivered of the spirit of suicide. He didn't kill himself, and neither did he retire.

GOD LOVES TO CHOOSE THE LEAST LIKELY HEROES. SO SPEAK OUT AND SPEAK UP, BECAUSE, TODAY, SOMEONE'S HERO JUST MIGHT BE *YOU*.

Let's never limit our expectations of what God can do because of our perception of anyone's situation. God loves to choose the least likely heroes. So speak out and speak up, because, today, someone's hero just might be *you*.

The Common Denominator: Someone Who Is Sanctified

Sanctification is an ongoing act of cleansing and consecrating our minds, hearts, and giftings to the Lord. Through this process, we set ourselves apart for God's use.

A Sanctified Imagination

Our imagination is a gift from God. As Christians, we should operate with a *sanctified* imagination. The word *sanctified* simply means pure, or clean.

Salvation goes beyond a verbal commitment to God. Once we are saved, the enemy battles to take us back. That's why we need to know we have access to the process of sanctification, or cleansing, whenever we may need it.

We have the power and authority to redirect our minds when they tend toward entertaining unsanctified thoughts involving such things as illicit drugs, alcohol, pornography, cussing, dirty thoughts and jokes, rude behavior, and so forth.

The enemy may try to plant ungodly thought-seeds in our minds, but we do not have to dwell or act upon those thought-seeds. The pastor of the church I grew up in told us, "Any bird can land on your head; it's up to you whether you let it make a nest or not."

How Do We Become Sanctified?

We are sanctified through the blood of Jesus. This happens through both our coming to salvation and our continually purging ourselves of unclean thoughts, desires, and deeds. (See, for example, Hebrews 2:11, 18; 13:12.)

This purging happens when we…

+ choose God's ways. This is a matter of making godly, right choices. (See 1 Peter 3:15; Romans 12:2.)

+ abide in God's Word, which continues to purge and purify us. (See John 17:17; Ephesians 5:26.)

+ continually cleanse our spirit, soul, and body from sin; and, when we do sin, being quick to repent and keep a short account with God. (See 1 Thessalonians 5:23; Isaiah 55:7; Titus 3:5.)

+ pray, carrying on a continual conversation and regular repentance with the Lord. (See 2 Chronicles 7:14.)

PRAYER

Father, please rid us of the view the enemy has given us of ourselves, and replace it with how You see us. Deliver us of condemnation and cleanse us of excuses. Please help us to soar in all You have to say about us. In Jesus's name, amen.

4

HOW GOD SPEAKS TO US

Let's talk about ways in which we might receive a prophetic word.

It may be that you have a slight impression, or a fleeting thought crosses the "radar" of your spirit, causing you to say, for example, "I had a feeling...." It's not a physical feeling; it's a spiritual impression. You may see a mental image as a still picture, or it may be a moving picture, similar to a video.

Another possibility is that you may receive a vision—something you see spiritually, overlaid on the natural scenery around you. Or, it may be an open vision, which causes everything in the natural to disappear, while you feel as if you have entered into that vision.

God also speaks to people through dreams.

It may be that words come to us even when we're not necessarily seeking them. These words can come no matter where we are or what we're doing. If you experience a seemingly random thought, or you receive a vision regarding someone specific, you should pray and ask God why, and whether He has a word for them. Always pray for that person's well-being, and then check on him or her if you feel so led.

When you begin to give a word to someone, the enemy may try to discourage you by causing you to feel crazy or stupid. He doesn't loudly announce, "Hey, it's me, the devil, and I have a thought for you to consider." If he presented himself so blatantly, you'd immediately reject his suggestions. Often, he makes himself sound like your own thought-voice so that you'll receive what he says. That's why we must be discerning and must know the

Word of God—that we may recognize the voice of condemnation as not being of God, and reject it.

Not every thought that comes to mind is from the Lord. But when we pray for a word for someone, we can trust that God will be faithful to give it to us. He will use us to encourage others, just as He has used others to encourage us.

Progressive Revelation and Interpretation

We know in part and prophesy in part. (See 1 Corinthians 13:9.) When we prophesy, we may receive only a few pieces of the puzzle. Sometimes, the completion of a message takes place over time, through interpretation, study of the prophecy and the Word, research, and additional prophetic words.

Prophesying in tongues usually occurs in a congregational setting during a time of worship in churches that permit this practice. The worship team will fall silent, yet those gathered will feel the Holy Spirit hovering near, searching for a willing vessel to deliver His message. Suddenly, someone will burst forth with a strong unction in an unknown language—a prophecy spoken in tongues. Such a prophecy requires interpretation, either by the one who spoke it or by someone else.

According to 1 Corinthians 12:10, the interpretation of tongues is a gift in itself. For some people, interpreting tongues is their primary gifting.

In the church where I grew up, God used a certain man to interpret tongues. This gentleman stuttered uncontrollably whenever he tried to talk in normal conversation, but the minute he began to interpret a prophecy spoken in tongues, he became articulate and even eloquent. No one doubted God was speaking through him when this happened.

If we sense that we have a message in tongues but not its interpretation, we are instructed by the apostle Paul to pray for the interpretation. God can give us both, according to 1 Corinthians 14:13–15:

> *Therefore let him who speaks in a tongue pray that he may interpret. For if I pray in a tongue, my spirit prays, but my understanding is unfruitful.*

What is the conclusion then? I will pray with the spirit, and I will also pray with the understanding.

Don't let not having the interpretation stop you from delivering a prophecy in tongues, as long as the Lord shows you that someone else can interpret.

How is it then, brethren? Whenever you come together, each of you has a psalm, has a teaching, has a tongue, has a revelation, has an interpretation. Let all things be done for edification. If anyone speaks in a tongue, let there be two or at the most three, each in turn, and let one interpret. (1 Corinthians 14:26–27)

I have been in congregational settings where there occurred a loud and long episode in tongues but no interpretation after. This sometimes happens. One possible explanation is that the person to whom God gave the interpretation became too shy or afraid to speak it. Another possible explanation is that someone grew too excited about a prayer in tongue that he or she blurted it out. In that case, no interpretation will occur. It's not a sin; the person simply misunderstood what was taking place.

The Prophetic Word Litmus Test

When you sense a word whose origins you are unsure of, consider running it through this prophetic word litmus test:

+ Do you have foreknowledge about it? If so, simply say, "I know (this) in the natural, but feel by the Spirit that God is saying (this) to you about it." Always be honest so that your integrity isn't hindered.

+ Does it agree with Scripture, or is it contrary to the Word of God? If it's the latter, pray against it and declare God's Word over the person.

+ Is it something you are able to interpret? If not, just describe the picture or words you have received, and say, "I have no interpretation, but this is what I received."

+ Are you supposed to give the word? If you aren't sure, ask God. Sometimes, the Lord gives us a word simply for the purpose of intercession. If it pertains to someone you will never see again, you should probably go ahead and give the word.

+ Is there a Scripture that matches the word? You might try typing into a Google search: "Scriptures relating to (topic)." The Word of God does not return void. (See Isaiah 55:11.)

+ Do you have a personal opinion of the person that may interfere? If so, simply pray a scriptural blessing over the person.

+ Be aware of and honor the prophetic guidelines set up by those where you are ministering.

+ Don't act in such a way that would turn others from our faith. Use good manners in the way you present a word. Being loud or showy isn't the anointing; it's just annoying.

+ Once you feel confident that the word you have received is from the Lord, go ahead and deliver it to the intended recipient. Move past your fears, and silence the enemy's lies. Every time you obey, the next time will be easier.

Our Plumb Line: The Word of God

All kinds of spirits exist, but we want to be sure we communicate with the *Holy Spirit*. Thus, God's Word must be our plumb line.

> *The Word of God is living and powerful, and sharper than any two-edged sword, piercing even to the division of soul and spirit, and of joints and marrow and is a discerner of the thoughts and intents of the heart.*　　　　　　　　　　　　　　　　　　　(Hebrews 4:12)

The more of the Word we digest, the more Jesus becomes a part of us. (See John 1:1, 14.) Spending time studying the Word of God also builds our powers of discernment. Hebrews 4:12 says that one of the Bible's functions is to discern, or divide, truth from falsehood. The Word within us will act as a two-edged sword, helping us to rightly divide the truth, while cutting off any soulish, ungodly parts.

You can ask the Holy Spirit to tell you the truth, and He will be faithful to do so. He is the Spirit of truth, after all. Jesus said the following about Him:

When He, the Spirit of truth, has come, He will guide you into all truth; for He will not speak on His own authority, but whatever He hears He will speak; and He will tell you things to come.

(John 16:13)

There have been occasions, while talking to someone, when I have prayed silently for God to prophetically reveal the truth—and, suddenly, a truth comes out of that person's mouth that astounds even him or her. These types of revelations are especially helpful when dealing with children or participating in counseling sessions.

How Do We Receive Words?

The Lord uses many different ways to reveal things to us. We may receive a Scripture verse, a song title or lyrics, a movie title or plot line. We may discern an area of gifting or potential employment, pick up on certain personality traits, sense someone's particular fear or joy, or see a vision like a flash. We may hear or see a word or a phrase. Or, again, a complete "motion-picture" scene may play out before us.

I got home late from a trip one night, my mind filled with thoughts of taking a trip to Israel. I had just talked with a friend who had recently traveled to Israel, and I was burdened knowing how much such a trip would cost me.

The next morning, I was awakened far too early, by loud music that I thought was coming from my clock radio. I couldn't get it to shut off, so I grabbed the plug and yanked it out of the wall socket. But the song kept going. I sleepily sat up on the side of my bed, thinking it was probably the neighbor's radio alarm.

The Lord, or maybe an angel, touched my arm and said, "Listen to the words! This song is for you." I quickly paid attention.

The song was "Time of the Season" by The Zombies—a secular tune, of course, but the lyrics struck a chord. The song talks of a "rich daddy" and of taking the listener to "promised lands."

I started shaking and crying as I screamed, "You're my Daddy! No one is as rich as You! I believe You're going to do it, Lord! You're going to pay for me to go to the Promised Land of Israel! Thank You, Jesus! Thank You! Praise You! I worship You! There's no one like You, Lord!"

If God can speak through a donkey, He can speak through secular songs to encourage us.

Someone unfamiliar to you may remind you of someone you know well. If this happens, God may be trying to tell you something about that unfamiliar person, such as a shared gifting or a similar trial being endured. Ask God to show you what He wants you to address.

If you are unsure how to proceed, it's always safe to just start praying for your recipient. If you open your mouth, God will fill it. (See Psalm 81:10.) That's called the *naba* word, which means to flow, spring, bubble up.[4] Just "let it rip" when the Holy Spirit takes hold of your tongue. This practice is a lot like praying in the Spirit.

God may reveal to you a detail about someone through that person's clothing or jewelry. You may pick up on colors, numbers, or symbols. You may have a sensing of a painful situation a person is going through. Your role is to pray, hear, see, then give the word, not doubting God.

A TRUE WORD FROM THE LORD WILL *NEVER* CONDEMN. NOR WILL GOD EVER TELL YOU TO PROPHESY ANYTHING CONTRARY TO HIS WORD.

Beware of any tendency to counsel, or you may overload the recipient of your word. Any true prophetic word is powerful enough to do what is needed.

A true word from the Lord will *never* condemn. Nor will God ever tell you to prophesy anything contrary to His Word.

---

4. http://biblehub.com/hebrew/5042.htm (accessed June 8, 2018).

Some Things Won't "Make Sense"

Not every prophetic word I've received has made sense to me, initially.

As we minister, the Lord will speak in such a way that the person receiving the word can relate to what is being said. The word may be conveyed with words you wouldn't normally use, or even in a language that is foreign to you. Don't measure God's messages according to your own understanding. Allow Him to stretch your faith to parameters that go beyond your own reasoning.

DON'T MEASURE GOD'S MESSAGES ACCORDING TO YOUR OWN UNDERSTANDING. ALLOW HIM TO STRETCH YOUR FAITH TO PARAMETERS THAT GO BEYOND YOUR OWN REASONING.

There may be times when we feel ridiculous as we act out a word God has given to us. Friends of mine felt the Lord telling them to plant fruit trees around their church, a congregation that hadn't seemed to bear spiritual fruit for several years. Wouldn't you know it, as the trees grew and bore fruit, so did that church. Sometimes, a simple act of faithfulness can reap great rewards.

At another friend's church, someone received a prophetic word about a clock. She began to pray and then acted out stopping a clock before it struck the top of the hour. The following day, in France, a clock at a school stopped just before the top of the hour, and thankfully so—a bomb had been placed in the clock, set to go off at the top of the hour. That person's prayers the previous night had saved many lives.

When you no longer seek to please people but only God, it won't matter to you what others think. It is then that you will see God work wonders.

The Libby's Commercial Word

I once spent three days teaching the prophetic contingency of a church. The pastor and his wife then asked me to offer prophetic presbytery for people by appointment in the basement of their home.

At one point, I had a slight break while I sat there waiting for my next appointment. In this moment, the song from an old TV commercial for Libby's vegetables popped into my head.

I snapped back to the present when I saw a young woman coming down the stairs. It was clear she was pregnant. She sat down in front of me, and I introduced myself, then asked her to wait until I had prayed for her before telling me anything about herself.

I sensed she had fear related to her pregnancy. I instantly saw a vision of three place settings. The hand of the Lord stretched out and motioned across them as I delivered a word that went something like this:

> The Lord showed me that you have fear about your pregnancy. However, I believe He wants you to know everything will be all right. Before you came down the stairs, I heard the old Libby's vegetable TV commercial song in my head: "If it says 'Libby's, Libby's, Libby's on the label, label, label, you will like it, like it, like it on your table, table, table." When I started to pray for you, I saw a vision of three place settings. Each setting had a plate, a bowl, tableware, a drinking glass, and a can of Libby's vegetables. The hand of the Lord stretched out and motioned across them, and He said, "Tell her she can have it—it's hers." I believe He wants you to know everything will be all right.

She was in tears as she got up to leave. She thanked me, saying she knew what the vision meant, but she didn't tell me any details.

A year later, I returned to the area, and some women asked me, "Did you hear what happened with that lady you sang the Libby's vegetable commercial to?" They then explained what I hadn't known at the time.

The lady had been to her doctor that morning and had learned she was expecting triplets. However, the doctor said that one of the babies was too tiny to make it, yet was stealing nourishment from the other two. He wanted the mother to "selectively reduce" (aka abort) the one that wouldn't make it. He explained that such a procedure could result in a total abortion of all three fetuses. The woman had then gone to see her pastor to ask him what to do. He said, "I don't know. But there's a prophetic lady at my friend's house, so perhaps the Lord would speak to you through her." Then sent her over to see me.

Because of what the Lord told this woman through me, she and her husband decided against a selective reduction. Within two weeks, all three babies were the same size. She carried them to term and delivered two girls and one boy, all of them healthy. Oh, yes—the lady's name was Libba. The Lord was calling her by the nickname Libby!

God knows what He's saying, so let's not second-guess Him. We must not allow our minds to be deterred by doubts or by the enemy's lies, lest we get so stuck dissecting things that we forgo speaking the words God gives us.

Hershey-Bar Breakthrough

At a Baptist church near Montgomery, Alabama, the pastor and his wife wanted everything the Lord had for the people they served—including the prophetic. They approached me at a meeting where we met, and asked if I would come teach and activate their group. I was also invited to stay in their home.

Before I go on, you should know that when I'm on the road, my digestive system tends to act up, resulting in constipation. For some reason, eating chocolate usually results in a "breakthrough" of this issue.

On my way to the meeting, I stopped at a convenience store to buy a bottle of water. At the checkout counter, I saw a Hershey bar on the candy display. I needed a breakthrough, but I resisted purchasing the candy bar because I had been following a low-carb diet.

In the church lobby following the meeting, the pastor handed me an envelope containing the money collected during the love offering. With a sheepish smile, he said, "Someone put a Hershey bar in the offering plate, so that's what you feel inside the envelope." I was stunned. "Oh," I said. "That's funny. Thanks."

That night, as I sat on the edge of the bed in the guest room at the pastor's house, I prayed, "Lord, thank You for the breakthrough I'm about to receive." I then ate the Hershey bar, asking God to bless the giver. Following my breakthrough the next morning, I went to the kitchen for breakfast with the pastor and his wife.

After the meal, the pastor said, "That was crazy that someone gave a Hershey bar in the offering."

I quietly commented, "Whoever did it really heard from God." I then related my story.

The pastor's wife started to cry. "It was me!" she admitted. "I stopped by the store to get things for kids' church, and I felt like the Lord said, 'Get that Hershey bar for Joni,' so I did. But I was too embarrassed to say that, so I put it in the offering plate!" She hadn't even told her husband what she had done.

I hugged her and thanked her for her obedience—and for my breakthrough.

A "Sense-of-Smell" Word

A family approached my prophetic team during a conference. I could sense that the man was dubious. Then I began to smell all sorts of coffees. I saw fleeting visions of him in airports around the world, and recognized that they were supposed to represent a series of business trips. I saw him buying bags of coffee and having them shipped to his home.

I saw on his face that he felt we were fake. I began to say something along these lines:

The Lord showed me that you're an 'I'm from Missouri, prove it' kind of guy. You don't buy into all of this. But God wants you to know it's real.

He showed me that you are a coffee connoisseur who travels on business trips across the globe. You try out various coffees as you go, having those you like mailed to your house. Then I saw you at home in your kitchen. You were grinding those whole-bean coffees, sniffing them to get the full effect of their savory smell. God said to tell you that He's letting you know this so that you will know this word is truly for you.

He wants you to know that He sees the desire of your heart to own your own business and to do things right, and that time has come. You are a man of integrity and have tired of the politics and unsavory business practices of others.

Habakkuk 2:2–4 is for you. Write your vision—even draw a rough draft of office blueprints. You will want that coffee area to be right, too. Then go for it.

The man broke down and cried. He then repented of his attitude and thanked us for going for it anyhow.

Steps to Take Before Delivering a Word to Someone

Before you start ministering prophetically, consider these directives:

+ Pray something like this: "God, I ask for a clear word for this person, like a sharpened, polished arrow, right to the heart of what's on Your heart. Please also give me a golden nugget to let them know that this word is truly for him or her."

+ Do a check of yourself—heart, mind, and body.

   a. Are you worried, depressed, angry, restless, lonely, fearful, etc.?

   b. Do you have any illnesses, aches, or pains?

   c. Do you have any unresolved conflict with anyone?

   d. If so, pray a cleansing prayer before going further.

   e. If not, and you sense any of these things, the issue may relate to whatever the person is dealing with. Ask God to give you pertinent encouraging words and Scriptures for him or her.

Pay attention to all your senses:

+ sight

+ smell

- touch
- hearing
- taste

Be Cautious of the Soulish Realm

We have this warning from God in Ezekiel 14:4–8:

*Thus says the Lord GOD: "Everyone of the house of Israel who sets up his idols in his heart, and puts before him what causes him to stumble into iniquity, and then comes to the prophet, **I the LORD will answer him who comes, according to the multitude of his idols, that I may seize the house of Israel by their heart**, because they are all estranged from Me by their idols."*

Sometimes, strong desires can turn into idols in the heart. Someone desiring to hear a particular word may press so strongly into the realm of the spirit to get it that you think you hear it, but it isn't from God; it's the voice of that person's soul and soulish desires.

This has happened to me. Once I realized what had happened, I felt defiled; I immediately retreated to my hotel, crying tears of repentance. I confessed to the Lord and asked Him to give me the wisdom and discernment to avoid doing that again.

Sometimes, people will pressure prophets in the soulish realm for a "matchmaking word." Don't fall prey to this tactic. Just because two people are single does not mean they belong together. Just because someone is single does not mean he or she should be married. We need to leave to God the job of pairing people up.

I've seen men "prophesy" to women they are attracted to in such a way as to connect to their souls. They lean in close, gaze deeply into these women's eyes, and tell them what wonderful, yet misunderstood, women they are. That's the hook. Later, they seek out these women, strike up a personal conversation with them, and try to start a dating relationship with them. One man I know would approach women in restaurants and use a supposed word from God as a pickup line. He would tap into her soul, get her to cry, sit down with her, and ultimately exchange telephone phone numbers with her.

Women can be guilty of this practice, as well. We must not defile ourselves or God's gift in this way. If you are attracted to someone, approach that person on your own merits. Don't misuse God. That's witchcraft.

A Word of Caution

When I was starting out in prophecy, I would sometimes mistakenly switch the words of two people sitting side by side, giving the wrong word to the wrong person. With the exception of spouses, the people to whom you minister should not have simultaneous physical contact with anyone.

Honing the Gift

It's important to be around other prophetic people to help identify things for each other. The spirit of prophecy heightens as we work together on our gifts.

Practice your gift as much as possible. Pray for servers in restaurants, shoppers at the mall, church members, coworkers, and your family members and friends who are willing to receive prayer. Pray for the churches you drive past, and consider dropping them a note. As with anything, the more you practice, the better you will get.

God speaks in many ways. Do the litmus test, then ask God to help you convey the word in order to bring life. Stop second-guessing yourself, and go for it.

PRAYER

Dear Lord, please help us to hear from You with greater clarity and faith. Use us to bring hope, faith, and encouragement to those we come in contact with, and to represent You faithfully. In Jesus's name, amen.

5

PREPARING FOR PROPHECY

Any worthwhile ministry we may do will come as a direct result of our personal relationship and walk with the Lord. We do not have to become professional speakers or ministers; we should seek to live in intimate relationship with Him, making ourselves continually available to Him. In the process, He will use the meager offering of ourselves for His glory.

Seeking affirmation and encouragement from people can become a snare. In order to avoid this snare, we must make sure that the Lord is our source—who we are and what we do.

Acts 4:13 says, "*Now when* [the crowds] *saw the boldness of Peter and John, and perceived that they were uneducated and untrained men, they marveled. And they realized that they had been with Jesus.*" Those who spent time with Jesus's disciples Peter and John, by observing their lives, could tell for a fact that those men had been with Jesus, because those men were changed as a result.

When we hang out with Jesus, it is evident. And it is just as evident when we don't. Pursuing the Lord changes us. We can't pursue Him without becoming different. (See, for example, 2 Corinthians 5:17.)

Some people seek to acquire the anointing vicariously, without making any personal investment. Receiving impartation by the laying on of hands at a meeting isn't a bad thing, but we won't receive the type of anointing that changes the world by going after someone else's gift. No, this anointing comes only when we establish a personal relationship with the Lord *for ourselves*. Again, He must be our main power source.

God can use anyone and anything for His purposes. After all, He spoke through a donkey when a man wouldn't obey. (See Numbers 22:28.) But by seeking to operate in the right spirit, we save ourselves a lot of heartache, rejection, and trouble.

Keys to Effective Delivery of Prophetic Words

Proverbs 18:21 says, *"Death and life are in the power of the tongue, and those who love it will eat its fruit."* We must be cautious of the way we speak prophetic words God's kindness brings the lost to repentance. (See Romans 2:4.) There is a proper time, place, and way to deliver messages of correction. The Lord's way of delivering these messages will bring life and hope, not condemnation.

We must trust God to give us a word for someone when we ask, and then believe Him enough to speak forth the word we receive.

It's important to give prophecies in a civil way. We should examine every aspect of how the word is handled before we deliver it.

One of the fruits of the Spirit listed in Galatians 5:22–23 is that of self-control. Therefore, we know that it is possible for us to convey prophetic words in a decent manner. We don't have to interrupt a service and holler out a word the moment we sense it. Prophetic words are not diarrhea. We should follow the apostle Paul's exhortation in 1 Corinthians 14:40: *"Let all things be done decently and in order."*

There's no need to be sensational, spooky, weird, or obnoxious; we need not speak in "King James English." We should operate in prophetic etiquette, not pathetic weirdness. One definition of *weird* is "of, relating to, or caused by witchcraft or the supernatural: magical." We don't need to be weird.

Our job is basically to act as spiritual couriers. Once we've delivered a word, our role is completed. We are not called to force anyone to receive a word or walk it out.

Also, let's not get trapped in the "paralysis of analysis." We need to step back and let God bypass our opinions, emotions, and run-amok minds.

God tells us, *"Open your mouth…and I will fill it"* (Psalm 81:10). Believe Him. As you begin to pray, it will loosen your tongue, similar to the act of praying in the spirit. Then, revelation will flow if you allow it to. It isn't coming from your thoughts; it's coming from the heart and spirit of God. Give Him the right-of-way.

AS GOOD STEWARDS OF GOD'S PROPHETIC
WORDS, WE MUST REMEMBER THAT ANY
WORD WE RECEIVE IS NOT *OURS*;
WE HAVE NO OWNERSHIP OF IT. GOD GAVE IT
TO US FOR US TO PASS ON TO THE PERSON TO
WHOM IT DOES BELONG.

As good stewards of God's prophetic words, we must remember that any word we receive is not *ours*; we have no ownership of it. God gave it to us for us to pass on to the person to whom it does belong. We must do our part, but what the recipient does with the word once we've given it is none of our business.

When we receive a prophetic word for someone, we are simply to be the delivery person. We are not to be anyone's substitute for the Holy Spirit. None of us is called to ensure that the person to whom we deliver a prophetic message follows through with what we have said. Sadly, many pastors have had to shut down the prophetic ministry in their churches due to this very problem.

Prophesy by the Spirit

It's important that we avoid ministering strictly according to what we see in the natural. Consider closing your eyes as you begin to pray for a person, that you might see more clearly by the spirit.

I don't usually seek to hear prophetic words for myself, but one time, while traveling, I approached a church's prophetic ministry team because no one there knew me.

Evidently, they could tell that I knew how to apply makeup, because one of them began prophesying along that vein, saying he saw me as a Mary Kay Cosmetics consultant. The entire word continued in that same vein, and absolutely no part of it proved accurate.

We must speak by the spirit rather than by sight, personal opinions, and best guesses.

Seek to Edify, Not Control

God's Word clearly tells us that we should seek to *edify*, or build up, the church, not to control it. As the apostle Paul wrote in 1 Corinthians 14:12, *"Even so you, since you are zealous for spiritual gifts, let it be for the **edification** of the church that you seek to excel."*

Too many times, prophetic people have acted as the church's spiritual police, using prophetic words to pressure pastors, church leaders, and others into carrying out their so-called revelations. That's charismatic witchcraft.

Our job is to carry out the heart and will of God, not to try to *be* God.

We must steer clear of controlling people, as well as from becoming controlling people ourselves.

There are three distinct types of control:

1. Manipulation (trying to trick others into doing something).

2. Intimidation (trying to scare others into doing something).

3. Domination (trying to force others into doing something).

Whoever we are trying to please, we have placed in a position of power over our lives. That is why it's crucial that we build healthy relationships, and surround ourselves with supportive, godly people. Along the same lines, we must avoid toxic people.

The Lord once told me, "Toxic people talk sick. They will pierce you in the heart of your purpose, call, and destiny, and kill it and you if you let them. So, don't."

Toxic people will divert our time, attention, money, and energy away from our goals, draining us of strength, life, and purpose. Therefore, we must associate with those who will be truthful but encouraging—those who "[speak] *the truth in love*" (Ephesians 4:15).

Offer Encouragement, Not Flattery

There's a big difference between flattery and prophetic encouragement.

Flattery is defined "insincere or excessive praise." Flattery is really a form of lying. It is a soulish practice that is sometimes used to manipulate other people, even if only to obtain their favor.

In contrast, prophetic encouragement is a true word from God that releases people from the enemy's control and propels them into the freedom to become who and what they were created to be and to do.

PROPHETIC ENCOURAGEMENT IS
A TRUE WORD FROM GOD THAT RELEASES
PEOPLE FROM THE ENEMY'S CONTROL
AND PROPELS THEM INTO THE FREEDOM
TO BECOME WHO AND WHAT THEY WERE
CREATED TO BE AND TO DO.

I once assisted in leading a regular women's meetings in someone's home. There was one woman—I'll call her Susie—who showed up late for every meeting. Each time Susie arrived, she would make noise and drew attention to herself. She had a "woe is me" attitude that prompted other people to ask her if she was okay. One particular day, her attitude affected the other women more than usual, and the meeting was blown completely off course as she played upon the ladies' empathy to draw them into her web. Before long, one of the other women had draped a blanket around

Susie's shoulders, someone else had given her a fireplace poker to hold as her scepter, and the others were actually stroking her arms and calling her their "queen."

I'd had enough. When it was my turn to speak, I removed the robe and took away the scepter as I said, "Now then, we *know* Susie didn't come in to interrupt and turn all the attention to herself, don't we? She doesn't want to be flattered or to be the center of attention, do you, Susie? We just speak into her that she can handle anything life throws her way, and she doesn't need us to feel sorry for her, right, Susie? She wants to encourage others, don't you Susie? There we go. Whom the Son sets free is free indeed. Now let's get back to the meeting."

After the meeting, I privately explained to the other leaders that Susie had been manipulating them with her actions. I then suggested they do a teaching on control and manipulation to enlighten the rest of the group.

Prophets are not supposed to stroke and pacify demonic strongholds but to get rid of them. Such situations call for discernment and action. When we discern the presence of a demonic stronghold and have enough strength of character to handle the related activity, deliverance can come as a result. We are to encourage people, not demons.

Exercise Discernment

Discernment is a vital tool in the belt of a prophetic person. It is the basis by which we determine whether a spiritual message we are hearing is from God or the devil. God's Word is our ultimate plumb line. God would never instruct anyone to do anything contrary to what He has told us in His Word. We must be lifelong students of His Word so that we may measure our revelation accordingly.

Proverbs 2:3 exhorts us to *"cry out for discernment, and lift up your voice for understanding."* *Merriam-Webster's Learner's Dictionary* defines *discernment* as "the ability to see and understand people, things, or situations clearly and intelligently." Synonyms include wisdom, insight, and perception.

The Bible warns us to be discerning of people. For example, we read in 1 Thessalonians 5:12, *"Recognize those who labor among you."* Perhaps everyone else is enamored of someone or something that causes you to feel apprehensive and concerned. Sure enough, the situation develops in such a way that it verifies your suspicion.

A lack of discernment can even prove deadly. Jesus gave us clear warning when He said, *"Behold, I send you out as sheep in the midst of wolves. Therefore be wise as serpents and harmless as doves"* (Matthew 10:16). He also warned us not to be ignorant of Satan's devices. (See 2 Corinthians 2:11.)

The moment we sense something isn't right is when we should realize that God is speaking by His Spirit to give us needed wisdom and discernment. This sense may come like a prophetic flash or a caution light. Whatever its form, we should slow down and pay attention.

That's why God's Word tells us, in Proverbs 2:3–11, to cry out for discernment. I once took this Scripture literally, and repeatedly cried aloud, "Discernment of God, come to me!"

A religious spirit will try to tell us that we are being judgmental, harsh, or ungodly if we are wary of someone. But the truth is that we are *not* to believe everything that presents itself as spiritual. Rather, we are to test *every* spirit. (See 1 John 4:1.)

We will even judge angels one day. (See 1 Corinthians 6:3.)

When we minister prophetically, we must make sure we are discerning and drawing from the proper spiritual source—that is, the Holy Spirit. We do not want to speak from the perspective of a person's soul, our own opinion, or the demonic realm.

Some people emit so much pressure in the soulish realm about their personal desires that we inadvertently pick up on those instead of on what the Holy Spirit is saying. If this happens, we may end up feeling sorry for that person, and prophesying from the realm of our own heart rather than from the realm of the Holy Spirit. In so doing, we would become like the prophets described in Jeremiah 23:16, who *"speak a vision of their own heart, not from the mouth of the Lord."*

There is no need to flatter or please anyone. Seeking God's counsel will lead us to speak words of truth that change lives forever.

As we seek His counsel, the words He gives bring salvation, healing, and deliverance—even eternal life. (See Jeremiah 23:18.)

Practice Humility

For I say, through the grace given to me, to everyone who is among you, not to think of himself more highly than he ought to think, but to think soberly, as God has dealt to each one a measure of faith.

(Romans 12:3)

Humility is key as we operate in the prophetic. We operate in humility by remembering where we came from and by refusing to become puffed up with pride over any gifting the Lord may have given us. Humility allows us to use what God has done for us to help set others free, too.

———

HUMILITY IS KEY AS WE OPERATE IN THE PROPHETIC. WE OPERATE IN HUMILITY BY REMEMBERING WHERE WE CAME FROM AND BY REFUSING TO BECOME PUFFED UP WITH PRIDE OVER ANY GIFTING THE LORD MAY HAVE GIVEN US.

———

Be Sensitive in Your Delivery

Oftentimes, it's not what we say, but how we say it, that makes a difference.

A friend of mine led a prophetic team with two other members, one of whom was a young student. An obese woman came in for ministry, and the student had a word about her having a good memory. He told her, "I see you like an elephant. An elephant never forgets." His wording proved offensive because he seemed to be insulting her weight.

Build a Trackable Record

We live in a time when many people practice their gifts without having demonstrated a trackable record. Therefore, it would be dangerous to restructure our entire lives around words that we do not bear witness to or whose timing has not yet come.

When I was a young single mother, I attended a meeting where several well-known prophets were ministering. The youngest and most inexperienced one called me out and prophesied that I would be married by the end of that year. The others judged and confirmed that they believed this word to be correct.

I did *not* get married by the end of that year. Absolutely no man came into my life, not even just as a friend. It doesn't matter to me now, but the disappointment of unfulfilled prophecy—or, rather, false prophecy—hurt my heart at that particular time.

That situation became an object lesson for the entire ministry to establish two rules: (1) Don't prophesy marriage, and (2) Don't prophesy using specific dates or time periods, as it is difficult to be accurate.

In my disappointment, I could have turned my back on prophecy. Instead, I allowed the experience to mature me. I took on the attitude of holding everything lightly in my hand. I would pray, "Lord, if this is You, breathe life into it. If not, blow it away." We are all learning, and none of us is 100 percent correct all the time. So, let's agree that we will not tar, feather, and mark as heretics those who err in their prophecies.

Conversational Prophecy

We can speak prophetically into the lives of others without telling them specifically that our message is from the Lord. There are many people who might think we are crazy, and would consequently reject our message, if we were to say to them, "The Lord wants me to tell you...."

In simple conversation, we can let others know what gifts we see in them, and encourage them that things will turn out all right. We know we are speaking by the Spirit, and the Holy Spirit will do His work in others through our words. Eventually, these individuals may "get it"; but let's meet them where they are rather than attempt to force-feed them with religious language.

Prophesying to Public Figures

When the Lord gives us an opportunity to speak to someone who is well-known or occupies a position of authority, we should keep the exchange private. The desire to receive attention for speaking to famous people can pose a real snare.

I cringe whenever I hear a speaker announce that he or she has just ministered to someone with a high profile. When the Lord grants us access to a public figure, we need to maintain confidentiality, not unlike a physician or other medical professional would do. In the case of political figures, it can cause problems for them if news of our encounters gains the attention of the mainstream media.

We should follow the example of Paul, who said, *"I went up by revelation, and communicated to them that gospel which I preach among the Gentiles, but **privately** to those who were of reputation, lest by any means I might run, or had run, in vain"* (Galatians 2:2).

God promises that He will bring us before *"governors and kings"* (Matthew 10:18)—in other words, people in authority. As we are faithful to cover and protect these people's identities and stories, more opportunities will come for us to minister to high-profile individuals.

During the time when I worked for a large church as the Singles Administrator and Single Parents Leader, the cousin of one of the single parents arrived from another country for a visit. I was asked to meet and minister to this gentleman at a local fast-food restaurant after church.

I prayed for the young man, and the word I received prompted me to tell him the following:

The Lord showed me you are unhappy where you live and are considering leaving. However, God says He has given to you great favor to eventually lead many people there. It is the enemy that is trying to discourage and make you give up. The things that upset you are on God's heart, as well. I saw you walking down the hallway of a government facility and sensed governmental authority on you. If you stay, the Lord will put you in place so that you will have the opportunity to make God-inspired changes in your nation that will cause it to be greatly blessed.

I don't remember the rest of our exchange, but I learned that this gentleman was a prince who had been seriously considering leaving his country. If he stayed, however, he would become king one day. He wept, bowed his head, and repented to God as he chose to go back home and lead his people.

By the way, if you are reading this and are a person in the public eye, please use caution as you decide whom to invite to minister to you, and how. You should always ask such people to minister to you in private.

One man had been given access to one of our nation's presidents. He began to post details about his visits on the Internet. He was called in to the White House, thanked for his prayers, and then told he could no longer visit with the POTUS. How sad. He had a genuine gift, yet he squandered the favor he had been given.

I have a friend in public office. He and his wife attended a local prophetic meeting, and the minister called out my friend, condemning him for a number of things that were untrue. My friend kept his mouth shut, but he had been terribly embarrassed in a public setting. He and his wife called me on their way home to tell me what had happened. I advised them to speak up immediately and set the record straight if anyone falsely accused him again. False information needs to be halted in its tracks before it spreads out of control.

I also suggested that if anyone tried to give him a word in public, he should stop that person and request that the word be given later on, in private. If the prophet were to have an issue with such a request, then his or her motive was clearly publicity, not ministry.

Giving Words to Children

It is best to speak over children in the presence of a parent, guardian, or minister—someone whom the child trusts who can help the child interpret the word and alleviate any related fears. This practice additionally provides protection for you.

Be just as gracious and nonconfrontational with children as you would be with adults, and do not speak any word that could become a burden to them. Remember, David was anointed as king while he was still a shepherd boy, and he continued living life as usual until his time came to take office. (See 1 Samuel 26:25.)

Be extremely cautious about ministering to children if you sense they may have been abused. Do not say anything to a child or a child's guardian that might endanger that child. In some cases, it is not wise to let them know what you see until help can be obtained. Be sure to immediately alert the church leadership about what you sense so that they can investigate and handle the situation with the proper authorities.

Small Word; Big Deal

During a Friday night School of the Spirit meeting at MorningStar, Rick Joyner directed us to give words to the guests. He called them up front and told us, "Go to whom the Lord highlights to you." I saw a lady and heard, "God loves you."

I thought to myself, *God loves everybody! I want a bigger word.*

Rick Joyner returned to the microphone and said, "God told me that one of my people said He gave them too small of a word, and they don't want to give it. He says if you don't, you won't get anything else."

With an apologetic spirit, I went to that woman and gave her the word. She immediately fell to the floor, crying uncontrollably.

Her hysteria went on for about twenty minutes. She finally explained that she'd had a conversation with God while driving over the River Bridge on her way to the meeting. She'd said to Him, "Nobody I know loves me. So, if I go to this prophetic place tonight, and nobody there tells me that *You* love me, I'm driving off this bridge into the river and ending it all on my way back."

Not such a small word after all.

God knows what each person needs. It doesn't matter how well off a person may look; it could be that he or she needs a word more than anyone else.

GOD KNOWS WHAT EACH PERSON NEEDS. IT DOESN'T MATTER HOW WELL OFF A PERSON MAY LOOK; IT COULD BE THAT HE OR SHE NEEDS A WORD MORE THAN ANYONE ELSE.

Be the Bridge; Don't Give Pathetic Words

People go through great atrocities, but the power of one word from God can change their lives forever. In many cases, a word from God can literally save lives.

We need to allow God to love others through us as we prophesy. Most people have been abused enough without our adding to the abuse in the name of Jesus.

A man labeled as a visiting prophet ministered at a friend's church and tore up the place with his words. He must have fancied himself as the church's version of insult comedian Don Rickles. Every word he gave contained degradation of some sort.

He called out one man as being ugly and asked him how he'd gotten such a pretty wife, saying maybe God felt sorry for him. Next, he called forth a young woman and insulted her outfit. He said she was pretty anyhow and told her God had a new job for her that paid well. He told her she needed to buy a new wardrobe with her first paycheck.

At another church, he continued taking similar cheap shots. He was so rude and distasteful that it's hard to understand why the pastors didn't stop him, let alone why they asked him to return. There's nothing funny about bullying people. Shepherds need to have enough boldness to remove someone from the pulpit the moment he or she begins hurting the sheep under their care.

PRAYER

Dear Lord, please give to us the wisdom and direction we need to hear and convey Your prophetic words accurately. Use us to encourage others to come closer to You and to hear from You for themselves. Please forgive us for doubting or drawing back when You give us a word that You want us to convey. Grant us the courage to go for it. Please also guard our tongues so that we might speak in a way that brings others life and freedom, and gives You glory. May we never take the glory for what You so graciously allow us to be a part of. In Jesus's name, amen.

6

THE ANOINTING AND THE GLORY

We can teach and pray for people until we are blue in the face, but if the anointing of the Holy Spirit doesn't show up, not much will happen. We don't want to just talk *about* the anointing; we want to *operate in it*. When the anointing comes, it breaks yokes and changes lives. Isaiah 10:27 says, *"It shall come to pass in that day that his burden will be taken away from your shoulder, and his yoke from your neck, and the yoke will be destroyed because of the anointing oil."*

Strong's Concordance defines *anointing* as "unction,"[5] "smear,"[6] "anoint,"[7] "anointed,"[8] and "fat, oil."[9]

In my earliest days of ministering, I felt shy and fearful; but once I opened my mouth to speak, the words would flow effortlessly. When the anointing came, even the bunny trails I traveled down in my conversations somehow fit in and ended up ministering to people. Prophetic words flowed like a river. When I would conclude, it was as if a balloon had popped and all the air had gone out; I would be "just me" again.

Without the anointing of the Holy Spirit, we are a bunch of bumbling idiots, accomplishing nothing—unless you count embarrassing ourselves.

When the Holy Spirit shows up, the anointing takes us beyond our limited, natural abilities and into God's limitless abilities. We become

---

5. *Strong's* Greek reference 5545
6. *Strong's* Hebrew reference 4886
7. *Strong's* Greek reference 5548
8. *Strong's* Hebrew reference 4899
9. *Strong's* Hebrew reference 8081

smeared and saturated with His supernatural power. Our ministry is fruitful because we no longer operate in our own strength but rather in His. The revelatory unction to prophesy takes on a life of its own. The Spirit works masterfully, like a well-oiled machine, to maneuver and minister from one person to the next.

I have also learned to pray that the Holy Spirit will anoint the ears of the hearers, as well. I pray that they will hear, understand, and apply what is taught. I pray for the breaking off of any yokes of bondage that may limit their ability to do so. That way, I am confident that when they leave my presence, the Holy Spirit will do His job of teaching and reminding them of what He has done. (See John 14:26.)

Gift of Administrations of the Holy Spirit

One of the gifts of the Holy Spirit is the gift of administrations. (See 1 Corinthians 12:28.)

From *Strong's* concordance, we have the definition of someone with this gift as "a steward, managing a household…"[10]; someone responsible for "affairs, service, work."[11]

The Holy Spirit knows how to manage the course of a service in God's house. To God's servants who will listen to His guiding voice, the Holy Spirit is the best GPS system there is. He maps out the best course of action as we simply follow His leading.

THE HOLY SPIRIT KNOWS HOW TO MANAGE THE COURSE OF A SERVICE IN GOD'S HOUSE. TO GOD'S SERVANTS WHO WILL LISTEN TO HIS GUIDING VOICE, THE HOLY SPIRIT IS THE BEST GPS SYSTEM THERE IS.

10. *Strong's* Greek reference 3622
11. *Strong's* Hebrew reference 5673

Like the best office manager, He skillfully designs every element of a program, from the worship, to the message, to the time of personal ministry. He knows the best timing for each. That's why, at my conferences, I tell the worship leaders in attendance to let Him guide them, and not to limit themselves by time restrictions. It is important to minister rightly to the Lord and to invoke His presence and direction. He inhabits the praises of His people (see Psalm 22:3 KJV), and so worship is the door by which He enters. The worship leader is the best judge of how to feel His leading in that arena. Why bother moving forward with the rest of the service until He arrives, receives, and is satisfied with our offering of worship?

Recognizing His Leading

A *knowing* comes with practicing time spent in His presence. The more we do it, the better we become at recognizing and knowing when we should move into another segment of a service. Sometimes, God wants to change the order of everything and have us remain in worship. We must not deny Him an extended time of worship if that is His desire.

Sometimes, if He wants to stress certain elements of a teaching, He may lead us along a path we hadn't planned. We may think we are off course when the "detour" is actually ordained by God. In such cases, it is not uncommon for someone to confirm the new direction by saying that he or she needed to hear the specific words that were spoken at that time. The Holy Spirit knew that.

Carrie Underwood's song "Jesus, Take the Wheel" comes to mind. If we want to produce fruitful ministry, we must not fear letting God take the wheel.

A Lesson

Years ago, while living in Kansas City, I was preparing to minister at a conference near Washington, D.C. Standing in my living room, I prayed, "Lord, everyone talks about being transparent. What does that mean? Am I that? Do I need to try more to be transparent?"

Suddenly, I heard a loud thud. I looked up at the sliding glass door leading to my patio. A dove had slammed into it and fallen to the ground.

"Oh, my!" I screamed, thinking my prayer had killed one of God's precious doves. It freaked me out because, in the Scriptures, the Holy Spirit is referred to as a dove. Thankfully, the bird got up and staggered away, alive.

"What on earth?!" I exclaimed.

Then, off to my right, a powerful gust of wind came in through my open kitchen window, blowing aside the sheer curtains. I stood with Holy-Ghost bumps on my arms, knowing a message would come. This is what the Lord spoke to me:

"It's not enough to be transparent. That sliding glass door is transparent, but nothing can come through it. I want you to be like that sheer curtain so that when the wind of My Spirit comes, you are willing to move aside."

The next day, I traveled by plane to attend the conference. The venue was the largest space I'd ever been invited to minister in, to date. I was both excited and apprehensive about the opportunity. Many speakers were lined up, each one given an hour, tag-team style. I was scheduled second on the afternoon list.

A young girl full of Holy-Ghost fire ministered first on the afternoon schedule. God moved mightily, and we all were captivated by the anointing on her.

Soon it would be my turn to speak. The conference director motioned for me to get ready.

The weather that day was warm, and someone had opened the windows near the ceiling of the auditorium. It was not particularly windy, but, suddenly, a powerful gust of wind blew through the building. I *knew* God was speaking through that gust of wind, and I also knew what He meant. He had prepared me in my living room for this moment. I was being tested. Would I move aside and let the wind of the Spirit continue to move through someone else?

Shaking under the power of God, I made my way to the conference director and whispered to her, "If it's okay with you and with her, I believe we are to let that young lady continue."

The director looked shocked. "Are you sure?" she asked me. "What if we can't fit you in anywhere else?"

"I'm here to see the Spirit move, even if it's through someone else," I replied, my words tumbling out. "I do not want to stifle what He wants to do."

We approached the young lady at the podium and whispered the idea to her. She was clearly surprised, and she asked if we were sure. I told her, "The Holy Spirit is sure."

THERE'S NO ROOM FOR COMPETITION IN THE KINGDOM. WHEN THE HOLY SPIRIT SHOWS UP, WE ALL WIN, NO MATTER WHOM HE USES.

The Lord moved so mightily in that next hour, not one person remained standing as His Spirit's wind blew through that place! In fact, the next speaker gave way to the Spirit's leading, as well.

There's no room for competition in the kingdom. When the Holy Spirit shows up, we all win, no matter whom He uses.

Imparting the Anointing

Many times, people will ask those in ministry to pray for them and to impart their anointing to them. While this *can* happen, what if someone receives an anointing but doesn't know what to do with it? What use is this practice if the gift goes unused in the recipient? We must be mindful of such things when people ask us for an impartation.

As an attentive student of the prophet Elijah, Elisha became Elijah's shadow. He traveled with and served him, watching his every move. His diligence earned him the right to receive Elijah's mantle. (See 1 Kings 19:21; 2 Kings 2:1–15.)

An element of impartation occurs when we serve under someone's ministry. We can recognize similar mannerisms that occur in a person's student as a result.

The most important thing is to stick close enough to the Holy Spirit to receive an impartation from *Him*. We are just the extension cord; He is the source.

The Armor-Bearer Thing

Some churches support the use of armor-bearers, or individuals who stick close to the leader in order to learn and receive impartations. The only problem is, in many cases, the leaders never actually train these individuals or allow them to "graduate." Instead, they treat the armor-bearers more like slaves than students, expecting to be waited on, hand and foot. And any armor-bearers who decide of their own initiative to move on are often marked as rebellious and end up being as good as excommunicated.

One woman had armor-bearers around her as she ministered, and she was acting so inebriated that the armor-bearers were carrying her from person to person to lay hands on those awaiting prayer. This woman moved like a wet rag. It was quite a show.

Let me just say that I don't think Jesus had to be held up and dragged around when He laid hands on anyone, and He *is* the anointing.

It's about time that we who are called to mentor others actually train, equip, and activate them to do ministry rather than assign them small, menial tasks meant to further our well-being. We should be loving spiritual parents, not spiritual slave masters.

When working with those you mentor, you should have them follow along with you down a prayer line, laying hands on and praying for people. Show them what to watch for. Question them as to what God is showing them. Teach them how to recognize various ways the Lord speaks, and to recognize how the Spirit guides and moves. Have them prophesy with you. Give them a few moments to comment on your teaching so they get used to being in the pulpit. Make them aware of the types of things they should watch for that may manifest, and teach them how to handle those situations. Equip them to serve God as well as those to whom they are called to minister.

Don't get me wrong, it's great to teach people to have the heart to serve. But I believe it's time for slavery in the church to end. We're called to raise up servants of the most high God, not servants of ourselves.

Is the Glory the Same as the Anointing?

God's glory is His alone and cannot be substituted by any person's idea of it. When it shows up, it means *He* has shown up. Nobody can promise God's glory will come. It's up to Him; it does not occur on demand. When His glory shows up, it isn't because someone waves his hand and announces it, but because God enters, and His train fills the temple.

It's difficult to define God's glory. You just *know* when it comes. The air becomes so saturated with the weight of His presence, it's hard to move, breathe, or talk. One feels as if he or she is being held in place and wouldn't dare to budge, even if it were possible. Along with God's glory comes an awesome reverence, a sensing that a greater power than anyone could ever imagine has just entered the room.

IT'S DIFFICULT TO DEFINE GOD'S GLORY. YOU JUST *KNOW* WHEN IT COMES. THE AIR BECOMES SO SATURATED WITH THE WEIGHT OF HIS PRESENCE, IT'S HARD TO MOVE, BREATHE, OR TALK. ONE FEELS AS IF HE OR SHE IS BEING HELD IN PLACE AND WOULDN'T DARE TO BUDGE, EVEN IF IT WERE POSSIBLE.

It's more than the anointing, which we can partake of and experience. God's glory *is* God Himself. And He doesn't need our help or our hype.

We see in Isaiah 60:1–2 that when God's glory and light arise upon His people, the process distinguishes His people from worldly darkness.

Once I asked God, "What is Your glory?" and He replied, "My glory is a changed life." When His glory comes, it alters lives eternally.

A Glory-Filled Lesson

I once ministered at a good-sized church in Vacaville, California. I taught one session and then returned on Friday evening to do a School of the Spirt meeting.

The worship had been incredible, and when the pastor called me up to minister, my sense of the Lord's presence was so strong that I could neither move nor talk. No one else could, either. Total silence enveloped the space. God's glory had entered the room. The pastor looked at me and mouthed, "What should we do?"

I whispered, "I saw Him moving among the people. I sure don't want to interrupt Him."

The pastor whispered back, "Me, neither. How long do you think we should do this?"

I said, "Until He's done." Then the Lord spoke a Scripture to me, Revelation 8:1 (KJV): "*There was silence in heaven about the space of half an hour.*"

Exactly half an hour later, I felt somewhat of a sense of release. The worship leader crawled across the floor to me and said, "I think I'm supposed to go up and begin to play the keyboard." The pastor and I agreed.

Finally, I felt the unction to get up and begin prophesying as God led me. I never did teach. It was an incredible night.

The next morning, when I arrived, the place was filled to capacity; it was standing room only. Word had spread that God had shown up. Testimony after testimony confirmed that the Lord Himself had walked among the people and personally ministered to them the previous night.

When God shows up with all His glory, it's not because we've done anything great; it's not because we've done anything at all. He simply comes and does what He chooses. It has nothing to do with us.

How He Comes

God can come as a rushing mighty wind (see Acts 2:2) or as a small, still voice (see 1 Kings 19:12). Regardless of His manner, there is no mistaking it is Him.

Jesus promised that He would send His Holy Spirit to be our Helper (see John 14:16)—the *"Spirit of truth"* (John 16:13), to anoint and to impart to us His power.

The Holy Spirit is the giver of gifts (see Hebrews 2:4), the presenter of fruit (see Galatians 5:22–23), and the power of God within believers (see 1 Corinthians 2:4). He can pray through us, anoint and work through us, or show up on His own. (See Romans 8:26–27; Acts 1:8.)

Let's listen and hear what the Spirit is saying to us, and work with Him to encourage and empower others in the kingdom.

PRAYER

Dear Lord, thank You for Your anointing that breaks the yokes of bondage off Your people. Help us to hear what Your Spirit is saying to the church, as well as to us, individually. May we all live to see and experience Your glory. In Jesus's name, amen.

7

WHAT TO DO WITH THE PROPHETIC WORDS YOU RECEIVE

Because we live in a time when all may prophesy (see Joel 2:28–29; Acts 2:17–18; 1 Corinthians 14:31), we cannot hold everyone who prophesies to the same standard as that to which the true Old Testament prophets would have been held. The Bible says that *all* may prophesy, not just prophets. The recipient of a prophetic word has the responsibility to judge, interpret, and walk out that word.

Basically, if a word doesn't bear witness with your spirit, you should either dismiss that word and never revisit it, or put it on the shelf and see if it makes sense at a later date.

Not every word we receive will confirm that which we already know. Often, a prophetic word is spoken to alert us that we have more potential inside us than we realize with our natural mind. Some people go through so many trials that they become "dumbed down" by the enemy as to their value. Through a prophetic word, the Holy Spirit may revive these people and bring them forth in their purpose, call, and destiny.

Receiving a prophetic word is the beginning of an adventure. Always do your best to record the word, or at least write it down as you receive it. If it is recorded, be sure to date it and type up any other identifying information for future reference.

When you receive a word, the first step is to discern whether it is in line with the Word, and if your spirit bears witness. If a prophetic word is contrary to the Word of God or makes you feel queasy and uneasy, go ahead and trash it.

Refuse Word Curses

I've experienced firsthand, and also heard horror stories of, supposed prophets or prophetic people speaking in an evil manner with their purported revelation. I've known some who can't discern their personal opinion from a prophetic word and will decimate others in the name of Jesus.

You know God's voice. If someone says something over you that is demeaning or sounds threatening, refuse it. Stop that person in his or her tracks and say, "I don't receive that." Waste no time in breaking the power of the faulty word using the authority you have been granted in the name and the blood of Jesus. Don't allow word curses to permeate your spirit.

The Creator of the universe crafted the world with His words. (See, for example, Psalm 33:9.) Since God is resident within every believer, our words also have creative power; *"life and death are in the power of the tongue"* (Proverbs 18:21). It is because of this that prophet Paul Cain once warned that we must exercise caution regarding what we bless as well as what we curse.

I always told my children to be careful how they spoke to one another, because good words create good things, and unkind words can have the effect of speaking a curse over someone. When my kids were about thirteen and fourteen years old, we experienced a real-life object lesson proving this point. We were in the process of packing up to move to a new house, and we had stopped to have lunch. I remember exactly what was on the menu: lunch meat, cheese, cheese doodles, nachos, and cheese dip. (Don't ask me why there was so much cheese.) After lunch, my friend Karen offered to take my kids and our pets to our new house while I finished cleaning the house we were vacating. We had a Labrador retriever named Spunky and a hamster named Harry, who looked like a miniature Sasquatch. For a *hairy* long-haired hamster, that name seemed appropriate. I had taught Harry to shake hands, sit up, beg, and do various other things. When I put my hand through the bars of his cage, he would lovingly rub his head against it like a purring kitten.

I hugged the kids good-bye, patted the dog on the head, and reached into the cage to pet Harry. I never thought about the remnants of cheese on my fingers, and Harry's being a rodent. Harry smelled the cheese and chomped down on one finger—hard. He would not release my finger, no matter what I did.

My son finally had the smart idea of offering Harry some real cheese. Harry released my finger and went for the cheese. I was so mad at him that I pointed my finger at him and scolded him, saying, "You're dead meat, buster!" My friend then left with the kids and our pets while I bandaged my wound and got back to work.

About thirty minutes later, the phone rang. "Joni, this is Karen," Karen said, sounding breathless. I could hear the kids crying in the background.

"Karen, what's wrong?" I asked. "Why are the kids crying?"

"The kids are okay, and I'm okay, but we had a little accident," Karen said. "The traffic light changed abruptly, and the truck in front of me stopped fast. I slammed on my brakes, too. The lady behind me wasn't paying attention, so she slammed into us."

"Oh, no!" I exclaimed. "Are you sure everyone is okay?"

"Yes, but I have bad news: When we got hit, the hamster cage tipped over, the hamster flew out, and the TV fell on top of him. I'm sorry, Joni, but Harry is dead."

I then heard the kids screaming in the background, "You did it, Mom! You cursed him with your words! You said he was dead meat, and now he is! You killed him!"

Life and death *are* in the power of our tongues. Thank God I didn't say those words to one of my kids.

We truly need to use caution regarding what we speak, not only over one another but also over ourselves. My older sister, Beverly, was always saying things like, "My head/tooth/stomach is killing me." At age thirty, one of her teeth abscessed and then drained through her bloodstream into her heart, causing acute endocarditis. She passed away, leaving her three boys motherless. Her tooth had literally killed her.

I'm not trying to scare anyone, only to stress the importance of rightly choosing the words we speak, especially when we are being used as God's mouthpieces to others. We want to speak words that bring life, not death. We want to be those who change the course of people's destinies so that they attain victory instead of defeat. We want to be the ones whom God uses to break the power of the negative words and curses that have been spoken over others.

The prophetic style of the last century, which relies on slander and embarrassment, will not set captives free. In fact, it does just the opposite: It *makes* captives, and it separates people from the church and from God.

At a church where I used to minister on a frequent basis, there was a female congregant who sold health supplements. Invariably, she would tell me that I *had* to take one of her products, or my health would fail. I ignored her for a while, but then she started saying that if I didn't take the products she sold, I would die. I drew the line and told her I refused her word curses. The last time I saw her, she handed me a note. She started to walk away, but I stopped her and then called the pastor over to look at the note with me. This time, the woman had tried to get away with cursing me with the written word instead of verbally. I refused her curse and gave the note back to her. She looked terrified and told me I couldn't do that. I said, "Sure, I can. You gave it to me, so I can give it to you." I later found out that she was a practicing witch.

WE DON'T NEED TO FEAR, BUT WE DO NEED TO USE CAUTION AS TO WHAT WE RECEIVE INTO OUR SPIRITS. DON'T HESITATE TO REFUSE A WORD SOMEONE SAYS OVER YOU THAT SOUNDS EVIL.

We don't need to fear, but we do need to use caution as to what we receive into our spirits. Don't hesitate to refuse a word someone says over you that sounds evil.

If you have experienced any of these things, pray and break their power off yourself now. Then go forward and leave them behind. They're over.

Interpretation

Once we've gone past the point of discerning the spirit behind a word, we move on to interpreting that word, as needed. Usually, a word is given in a manner that is understandable; but there are times when words are conveyed in the form of pictures or dark sayings. That's when we need interpretation.

It may be that those who give you a word speak through symbolism. While they may have their own interpretation of what the word means, you should pray over it and see what God gives to you about it. It's *your* word. Some words given to you can be interpreted by you alone, because God often speaks to us in a language and form that we alone understand. God loves to give us little golden nuggets of proof like that so we might know they are truly for us. The person prophesying won't understand that. Therefore, pay attention to any special terminology that may come within a word. If you get stuck regarding the interpretation, consider exploring some books on the topic. Kevin Conner and Ira Milligan have some very good resource material with information on the meanings of colors, animals, signs, and other symbols.[12]

It's also a good idea to have someone you trust, such as a pastor or another spiritual overseer, help you discern a word.

Application

Once you have a solid interpretation of the word, you are then responsible for taking the appropriate action. Applying a word is an act of faith. Sometimes, seeing a word come to pass is a simple matter of waiting on what's been spoken. But rarely are words fulfilled instantaneously or with

12. See Kevin J. Conner, *Interpreting the Symbols and Types* (Portland, OR: City Bible Publishing, 1980), and Ira Milligan, *Understanding the Dreams You Dream* (Shippensburg, PA: Destiny Image Publishers, 2010).

no requirement of action on our part. Just as a baby doesn't instantly appear, there is usually a "gestation period" for the prophetic words we receive. Many of the words I received took twenty years or more to come to pass. Don't give up on the brink of your miracle by word-cursing it with something like, "Forget it! It will never happen!" You can have what you say. Often, a personal prophetic word requires some type of movement toward that goal on our part—in which case, if we do nothing, then it will not come to pass.

Just because we receive a nice prophecy doesn't mean we are perfect. The woman caught in adultery by Jesus wasn't perfect. God often uses such a word to encourage us to walk out of sin and into our purpose in Him.

Timing Is Everything

With many prophetic words, timing is of the essence. We may see the big picture, like the lid of a puzzle box; but many tiny pieces must come together before we see it materialize fully. Through faith and patience, we inherit the promises. (See Hebrews 6:12.)

DON'T DEBATE WITH DEVILS! IGNORE THEM AND THEIR FOOLISH SPIRITS OF CONDEMNATION, LIES, AND DISCOURAGEMENT. CAST DOWN THOSE IMAGINATIONS, AND BEGIN TO SPEAK LIFE TO YOUR PROMISES.

The enemy of our souls would love to have us operate in soulish reasoning to the point that we would give up on the promises of God. He wants us to believe that the things we are believing for will never come to pass. We must be smarter than him. Don't debate with devils! Ignore them and their foolish spirits of condemnation, lies, and discouragement. Cast down those imaginations (see 2 Corinthians 10:5 KJV), and begin to speak life to your promises. Thank God that you are another day, week, month, and year closer to the fulfillment of those promises than you were yesterday. And once you know you've done everything in your ability to bring a word to pass, simply *stand*. (See Ephesians 6:13.)

Personal Prophecies Are Often Invitations

My life changed when I came to understand 1 Timothy 4:13–16 and realized that some of my prophecies hadn't come to pass because I hadn't done anything about them. I discovered that many prophecies are an invitation that we must pursue in order to see the promise manifested.

Most of the time, we will have to *do something* in order to move closer to the fulfillment of a prophetic word.

MANY PROPHECIES ARE AN INVITATION THAT WE MUST PURSUE IN ORDER TO SEE THE PROMISE MANIFESTED. MOST OF THE TIME, WE WILL HAVE TO *DO SOMETHING* IN ORDER TO MOVE CLOSER TO THE FULFILLMENT OF A PROPHETIC WORD.

Take a look at the Scripture passage that brought me to this revelation:

Till I come, give attention to reading, to exhortation, to doctrine. Do not neglect the gift that is in you, which was given to you by prophecy with the laying on of the hands of the eldership. **Meditate** *on these things;* **give yourself entirely to them,** *that your progress may be evident to all. Take heed to yourself and to the doctrine. Continue in them,* *for in doing this you will save both yourself and those who hear you.*

(1 Timothy 4:13–16)

The phrase *"give yourself entirely to them"* hit my spirit with the force of a cannonball. I hadn't done anything toward my promises before then, because of a false teaching I'd heard that said, "If the word is from God, it will come to pass, and you don't have to do anything about it."

The truth is that faith without works is dead. (See James 2:17, 20, 26.) If we believe God, we will go for it.

Confirmation or Not?

While it is true that some words are meant to confirm that which you already know, that is not always the case.

You could never have convinced me that some of the prophetic words spoken over me were for real. I honestly thought the people giving such words to me were crazy when they spoke of my being in ministry, training ministers, and speaking to government leaders. As a single mother struggling to raise two small children on my own, I wondered how on earth could they think such things would come to pass. Thank goodness my doubting thoughts weren't visible to the ones prophesying! They would have seen such thoughts as, "That guy is crazy," and "That dude has the wrong number."

I believed all sorts of demeaning lies about myself, until I got delivered from rejection and self-condemnation. When I began to receive those words spoken over me, time and time again, they finally soaked in to the point that I started to believe them instead of believing the lies of the enemy.

Once I finally got it, I developed the desire to help others discover the truth about themselves, as well. I prophesied hope over anyone or anything in my path: people, churches, nations, furniture, the family dog, my front door—you name it.

God uses prophetic words to bring deliverance from the lies of the enemy and to instill His truth in us. Because of what He has done for me through His prophetic encouragement, it has become my life's passion to be His tool to do the same for others.

Write Out the Words You're Given

I watched an interview with New York businessman Donald Trump before he became our nation's president. In it, he was asked whether it is important for people to set goals and, if so, why. The interviewer also asked him to define the difference between those who set goals and write them down, and those who do not.

Mr. Trump replied that it is vital to set goals as well as to write them down. He explained that those who set and write down their goals will achieve them, while those who do not will never succeed.

I once worked for a company that sent us into businesses to help the business owners develop goals for themselves and their employees. We used a packet to help the business owners write out their goals in attainable increments, and the process was a real eye-opener for me. It set a pattern for success in my life, helping me actualize what God had promised.

IF WE WANT TO ACTUALIZE THE PROMISES OF GOD, WE MUST BELIEVE HIM ENOUGH TO GO FOR IT. THAT'S JUST HOW IT WORKS. IT'S TRUTH AND IT IS SCRIPTURAL.

We can receive by faith all the words anyone could ever prophesy, but, again, faith without works is dead. If we want to actualize the promises of God, we must believe Him enough to go for it. That's just how it works. It's truth and it is scriptural. As the apostle James wrote, *"I will show you my faith by my works"* (James 2:18).

Setting goals has become a part of every aspect of my life. Writing a shopping list that I refer to at the store helps me to avoid wasting time and money, since I don't need to return to the store for any forgotten items. Writing a list of my monthly bills has helped me to stay on budget. Writing a list of daily tasks has aided me to properly budget my time, enabling me to accomplish more. Putting our goals into writing truly sets things in motion, naturally and spiritually.

Jeremiah 30:2 instructs us to write in a book all that we have been told by the Lord. In other words, we should keep a journal—a trackable list of the revelation we have received from the Lord.

As Habakkuk 2:2 tells us, we need to write out our vision so that we have it in front of us as a road map to follow.

Pray Over Your Promises

Keep up with the promises God gives to you. Speak life into them by praying over them. Work your way toward them. Even enlist a trusted friend to help remind you of them.

You should be very selective about the people with whom you share your dreams, your heart's desires, and the prophetic words you receive. Tell them only to those you fully trust. Don't be like Joseph, who told his brothers his dreams, causing them such jealousy that they sold him into slavery. (See Genesis 37.) All too often, we share things with people who smile to our face but then stab us in the back once they walk away. Find trustworthy friends with whom to share your treasures.

I never would have dreamed that some of the people I trusted would betray and mock me behind my back. Don't cast your pearls before swine. (See Matthew 7:6.) Some people desire to hear information just so they can give it out. Don't share your personal information with any "information junkies" who will "get high" on publicizing it and tearing you apart.

Jealousy is a terrible thing that can come from the most unexpected of sources. Its daggers can go deep. Don't expect demonic spirits to be happy for you. If you receive a word spoken over you in public, cover yourself and that word in the blood of Jesus. Pray that any hindering forces won't even hear, let alone remember, what was spoken over you.

Don't Be a Prophecy Junkie

In one town where I ministered, people followed me around and got in line for another prophetic word at each venue. Something about their persistent pursuit gave me the creeps. I started to feel that these people viewed me as a woman who reads crystal balls. I prayed, and the Lord directed me to establish a rule that there was to be no "double dipping"; each person would be prophesied over only one time.

The Lord showed me that we will stand before Him and be held responsible for all the words we have received. He does not desire to give additional instructions to those who have not followed the instructions He's already given them. Therefore, He wanted me to use caution and to speak only over those individuals whom He told me to speak over. Thus, I quit having prayer lines where everyone received a word, and started speaking only over those whom He led me to during a service.

WE CAN ALWAYS RECEIVE WORDS FOR
PEOPLE, BUT WE SHOULD NOT ALWAYS GIVE
THOSE WORDS TO THE PEOPLE CONCERNED.
WE SHOULD NOT TREAT GOD'S GIFTS
DISRESPECTFULLY BUT SHOULD DO ONLY
WHAT THE FATHER SAYS TO DO.

We can always receive words for people, but we should not always give those words to the people concerned. We should not treat God's gifts disrespectfully but should do only what the Father says to do.

In certain places, the Lord has shut me down from giving *any* prophetic words. He has had me tell the people that they need to go back over the words they have already received and be faithful to act on them.

The bottom line: Prophecy isn't a game. We are dealing with the Holy Spirit. He is *holy*. We need to respect Him and His gifts, not operate in ways that are akin to fortune-telling and divination.

I write this not to condemn anyone who may have misused God's gifts in the past. We all live and learn. I can't say I have always done the right thing. Reflecting on some of the things I've done, I'm thankful that the Lord was patient and merciful with me, and that He helped me learn how to do things better as I went along. In fact, I'm still learning.

PRAYER

Lord, thank You for the words You've already given to us. Help us to go through them, chewing up the meat and spitting out the bones. Show us the prophetic words we need to give ourselves to, and how to do it. We will be sure to honor You for any good thing accomplished. In Jesus's name, amen.

8

PROPHETIC CORRECTIONS AND WARNINGS

Prophetic correction is a touchy subject. Some people believe it should never be done, while others feel it's their personal calling. In this chapter, I will endeavor to bring some balance to the topic.

When the prophetic begins operating in a congregation, corrective words will usually rise from multiple sources. Most of these words end up being personal opinion, not God's truth. For pastors, it is crucial to establish a list of guidelines for dealing with such "words." Otherwise, they are in for a big mess.

First of all, let's discuss manners. Any corrective words you sense for someone specific in a church congregation should first be brought before the pastor in a private setting. When I'm ministering at a church and I notice a potential problem with one of the congregants, I am cautious regarding how to address the issue, keeping in mind that the church is not my own house. One guideline that was emphasized by those who trained me was this: If someone is not in your area of responsibility, then it is not in your area of authority to personally correct that person. Any words of correction should be taken to those in authority over that person.

Be mindful of the way you convey what you have noticed. You aren't there to divide and destroy. Be aware that if that pastor decides to address whatever it is that you have told him, he may reveal your identity to the person concerned. In some cases, he may even request that you attend a meeting with that person. Make sure you are prepared to become involved in that way.

Ask God if and how you are to address the issue. Do it properly, giving wise counsel with biblically sound options on how to handle it. Then, be prepared for any personal fallout that may occur as a result.

A Note to Pastors

Pastors, make it clear that anyone with a corrective word must present it to the church leadership in a responsible manner. Make it plain that anonymous words will not receive any credence. The person giving the word must type it up, print it out, date it, and sign it, being sure to include his or her contact information. Then, he or she must give the printed document to the appropriate person in authority, and make himself or herself available in case any questions should arise. Let the person know that this process is important for preserving integrity. On the upside, if the warning proves accurate, that information will help develop a trackable record for the giver of the word.

If one of your watchmen or a visiting minister picks up on something that is potentially harmful to you or your congregation, be sure to see if everything lines up before you act upon that word. Seek God's help to rightly research, judge, and handle it.

Next, protect your sources from any potential fallout related to that word. Do not call in the person named in the warning and tell him or her, "Sister So-and-So gave me a word about you and said...." As the shepherd of your flock, you need to protect *all* your sheep. If you address the situation at all, address it on your own merit.

Sometimes, God prophetically shows us something corrective solely for the purpose of prayer. In that case, as we pray, the Holy Spirit will convict the person's conscience, and his or her life will be changed without our doing anything else.

Why Correction?

Let's suppose that you receive a genuine corrective word from the Lord—a word that may save or protect someone's life or soul.

In this era of seeker-friendly, people-pleasing churches, too much has been let go. God forbid that any message tell the truth, lest someone become offended. But what does the Word have to say about that? "The wise of heart will receive correction." (See Proverbs 10:8.)

We have no business correcting others as a matter of personal opinion. However, if a life or a soul is at stake, and we receive a word that pertains to the situation, it's our obligation to speak forth that word. The gravity of withholding a God-given warning is laid out in the book of Ezekiel:

> *When I say to the wicked, "You shall surely die," and you give him no warning, nor speak to warn the wicked from his wicked way, to save his life, that same wicked man shall die in his iniquity; but his blood I will require at your hand.*   (Ezekiel 3:18)

How we address corrective words matters. We should convey them in a loving way, for it is God's kindness that brings us to repentance. (See Ephesians 4:15; Romans 2:4 NIV.)

That doesn't mean we should be wishy-washy. We can speak the truth firmly and in a loving way. Our motive should never be to shame or humiliate anyone, but rather to reconcile them to the God who loves them just as He loves us.

WE CAN SPEAK THE TRUTH FIRMLY AND IN A LOVING WAY. OUR MOTIVE SHOULD NEVER BE TO SHAME OR HUMILIATE ANYONE, BUT RATHER TO RECONCILE THEM TO THE GOD WHO LOVES THEM JUST AS HE LOVES US.

Confrontation will sometimes cost us a friendship. That's the chance we have to take, because confrontation may save a life or a soul.

Brethren, if anyone among you wanders from the truth, and someone turns him back, let him know that he who turns a sinner from the error of his way will save a soul from death and cover a multitude of sins.

(James 5:19–20)

Personal Examples

A Workplace Event

At one of the international ministries where I have worked, each department met for staff devotions for the first thirty minutes of every day. At the time, I was a young single mother. As I got ready for work one morning, I had an experience with the Lord. Like an audible voice in my spirit, He said, "I want you to go to every department and give them a message this morning. Tell them to stop destroying the ministry from within by the words of their mouths. I will take care of the leader. Their responsibility is to do their jobs as unto Me, not to destroy him or that place with the words of their mouths. Go to all other areas first, then lastly to your own area's vice president and your office."

I said, "But, Lord, I'll get fired. I'm a single mom and the sole support for my children."

Suddenly, I saw an open vision. Stretched out before me was a path that reminded me of the yellow brick road in *The Wizard of Oz*. This heavenly street of gold led to God's kingdom at the end. God said, "Are you working for them or for Me? Seek first *My* kingdom and *My* righteousness, and I will give you all you need."

So, I did as He said. Scared and shaking, I delivered the message to each department, moving quickly so I could finish before possibly being fired. When I arrived at the office of our area's vice president, I rushed past the secretary, who jumped up to stop me. However, I had already begun to speak to the vice president. He turned ash white, making me more afraid. He grabbed my hand and led me across the hall to my own office area, where he interrupted the staff devotions and had me give the word.

Meanwhile, behind him, the heads of all the departments I'd already spoken to had lined up, looking ready to complain about me. This vice president didn't see them, however, and he told me that he wanted me to go to every department and deliver the word. I told him that I had already done so. I explained that God had told me to do it that way, ending with our own department.

He asked, "What did the others do with it?"

I said, "I don't know. They are standing behind you in the doorway, so I guess you can ask them."

He turned around then and commanded all of them to return to their departments and to call for a time of fasting and praying until noon. "Get everyone to pray as this handmaiden of the Lord has said," he told them. Then he faced me once more, falling on his knees and putting his hands on my feet. He prayed over me, saying, "God bless this handmaiden of the Lord! Thank You for her courage!"

I later discovered that he had planned a confrontational meeting with the head of the ministry that very day. His intention had been to issue an ultimatum that could have destroyed the ministry immediately if the leader had refused to do what was demanded. God changed his heart, and unity was fostered between him and our leader that day.

Later that afternoon, I learned that those who had been angry at me for what I had said had tried to have me fired. They were fired, instead. I didn't rejoice in the news but rather felt the awesome fear of the Lord come upon me.

Bringing a Friend Back to Jesus

Chris and I had been friends for many years. We had worked together, gone to church together, and spent many good times together with our families.

Through the years, Chris had endured a lot of heartache. After a third failed marriage, she decided she wouldn't marry again; she would just live with a guy. She knew better, but she had been severely wounded. At one point, Chris had been a pastor's wife, but even he had cheated on and then left her.

One morning, as I woke up, the Lord spoke powerfully to me about her. He said, "Call Chris. Tell her I love her, and I'm jealous over her. It's time for her to return her heart to Me."

I said, "God, I love her. She is like a blood sister. What if she gets mad at me?"

He said, "I love her, too. Because you *do* love her is why I chose *you* to go to her, because I know *you* will do it with My heart and love."

I felt nervous, but I prayed and then picked up the phone.

"Chris," I began, "I called you for a reason. I just hope you know how very much I love you. You are like a sister to me."

She said she felt the same, then asked me what was wrong.

"Chris, you know I have never put you down for anything you've done. I understand, because I've seen what you went through—and I'm not condemning you now. But, Chris, I had a visitation from the Lord about you this morning." I couldn't help it; I began to cry. "Chris, God said to tell you that He loves you very much, but He is jealous, and He wants you back. He said it's time."

There was silence for a moment, and then I could hear her weeping.

"Chris, please don't be angry at me," I continued. "Please don't think I'm putting you down. I love you. God loves you. That's why He's jealous and wants you back. And I want you back, too. Eternally. This was so hard for me to do, but I want to know that I will spend eternity with you as my friend. Please come home to Him. Please?"

Both of us were weeping.

Then Chris said, "I know this was hard for you. I love you, too. I'm not mad. Thank you for caring enough to be so brave. It's confirmation. Every time I pass the little church near me, I feel like it's reaching out to me. I thought I was crazy, just wanting it to be true. But now I know it's true. I'm going to go there and get my life back together."

And she did. She attended a service and went forward for the altar call. She continued going there regularly and soon joined the Bible study group of that loving little church. She became happy in the Lord, like the friend I'd long known.

A few months later, I received a call. Chris had been in a terrible one-car accident. Her vehicle had rolled over, killing her.

I wept hard but felt very thankful that I'd obeyed the Lord and helped lead my precious sister back to Him. I knew for sure that she had gone to heaven.

A Wild Night

One night, I ministered at an inner-city church in Montgomery, Alabama. The area was so rough, even ambulance drivers requested a police escort. When my sponsors and I arrived, the church sent out six big bouncer-type men to surround and lead us safely indoors.

The pastor was a wild man. I never go by a title, but he hollered, "The prophetess is here! Tell us the way it is! Correct us publicly, if you have to! We receive you, prophetess!" and other such things. He also introduced me to various people, including his wife and his secretary.

Later, I had a few questions, so I went to look for either the wife or the secretary, but I kept getting confused. Finally, I prayed, "Lord, help me. I keep getting confused as to which one is the wife and which one is the secretary."

He said to me, "I know. So does the pastor."

Whoa!

After the teaching, The Lord led me into a time of prophetic ministry. It went something like this....

"Where is the pastor's secretary? Oh, there you are. You're a single mama, aren't you? And you desire to have a mate, right? Well, the Father says, your husband is *not* in *this* place. Do you understand me? He is *not* in *this* place. You have an opportunity to live with relatives in another city and go to school there. That's where you will find your husband. But he is *not* in *this* place. Do you understand what I'm saying?"

She turned red and nodded her head yes. She understood the implication—that her husband was *not* the pastor.

Then I asked the pastor and his wife to come forward. I began, "The Lord has called the two of you as a team. Pastor, He will only give you authority with *His* bride to the degree that you properly take care of *your own*. To do less would be to condone spiritual adultery.

"He says He has canceled the enemy's assignment against your marriage. It's now time to take a vacation—a second honeymoon. No, it's a first honeymoon, as you never took a first one. And it's time to reconnect as He has meant you to.

"Do not minister to women without your wife's being present. God has given her great discernment. Her presence with you will thwart the enemy's plan to allow a woman to take advantage of your compassion and thereby destroy the team of the two of you that God has ordained in this place."

What a powerful night of encouragement! God brought loving correction *within* the encouragement.

Prophetic Team Experiences

I was ministering with a prophetic team during a conference when three women came in and I heard, "Witches of Eastwick." I had never seen the movie *The Witches of Eastwick*, nor had I read the book by the same name; but I assumed the phrase meant that these women were witches. The rest of my team members gave great words to the women, but I sat there thinking, *Are you crazy? Can't you see that they are witches?*

The Lord suddenly broke in and said to me, "You are the one who's wrong. These three women are not witches but precious intercessors who are under an attack by witches in their area. Pray those curses off of them."

That experience taught me to use caution when tapping into the spirit realm. I had heard the false accusations being spoken against those three women. Thankfully, the Lord corrected me before I spoke in error.

Another time, I was serving on one of my church's conference prophetic teams when a married couple came in. Every time the husband would try to speak, the wife would take over and speak for him. It was funny but also sad.

To be honest, I became frustrated with the wife. But God had the right way to handle it. He told me that if I would just open my mouth, He would fill it. What He gave me to say went something like this:

> The Lord showed me that you married very young. Sir, because you didn't have an example to follow of how to be a husband who takes care of things, your wife had to. Ma'am, God said you've been praying for years for your husband to step into his rightful place. However, you are so close to the situation that you haven't seen that it's already happened. Even here, you are so used to speaking for him that every time I asked him something, you replied for him. God says, sir, He sees the rich deposit inside of you and even the teachings ready to burst forth from you. He says it's time. Ma'am, He says if you will step back and listen and let him speak, you will realize you have the man you've prayed for him to be.

They both wept for joy. It was awesome. God brought correction *and* deliverance in a loving way.

A Funny (True) Story

When I was about ten years old, my family lived in Southern California. My older sister and I went to the grocery store one day and saw a man approaching us in an aisle, and I had a flash vision that he drank alcohol in excess and also abused his family. So, I started yelling at him: "Hey, mister! You better stop getting drunk on beer and abusing your family! God is going to get you for that! He sees what you are doing, and you are in trouble!"

Mortified, my sister grabbed me and began trying to drag me away, all the while saying to me, "Shut up! You don't know that! Stop that right now!"

I broke loose from my sister and ran after the man, getting in front of him just as he picked up an armload of beer. I kicked him in the shins and screamed at him again, "God sees what you're doing! You better listen, or God is gonna get you!"

The whole time, the guy said absolutely nothing; he just stared at me. I don't know what ever became of him.

By the way, I've since learned that's *not* how to do things.

God still uses the prophetic for edification, exhortation, and comfort, even in the area of correction. (At least when we are grown up enough to understand that.) He *is* love. *Love wins.*

PRAYER

Dear Lord, thank You that You care enough to bring correction when we need it. Help us remember to operate in Your love when You call on us to deliver words of correction to others. May we be found faithful to speak from a heart filled with Your compassion. In Jesus's name, amen.

9

TYPES OF PROPHETS AND PROPHETIC MINISTRIES

Just as there are many ways of seeing and perceiving in the natural, there are different manners of viewing things prophetically in the spirit realm. In the early days of the prophetic training I received at MorningStar Ministries, I felt left out because I received revelation in a different way than anyone I knew. I saw video-type visions and words, while everyone else saw pictures. While other people talked about the pictures they had received, I would see words spread as if across the bottom of a television screen, similar to closed captioning, as an interpretation of the picture.

I didn't understand what was happening until God used Rick Joyner to help reveal and explain that I had a gift of interpretation. Additionally, Prophet Bob Jones told me, "You're a seer like me." Thankfully, he mentored me weekly for five years and helped me to understand my gift. I also attended several prophetic training modules at Bishop Bill Hamon's ministry, Christian International, where I learned how to tap into the naba prophetic flow—a term I will now explain.

Types of Prophets

Different types of prophets are more anointed than others in certain areas. This does not mean that prophets cannot receive information in ways other than their primary manner, only that they have a unique *specialty*. While the following categories aren't exhaustive, they will give you a basic idea of several primary types of prophets at work on the earth today.

Naba Prophets

Naba means "to prophesy,"[13] "to flow, spring, bubble up,"[14] "a prediction (spoken or written)."[15] The naba prophet does not see or know anything until he or she begins to pray or speak over someone. Naba prophets operate on the premise of God's promise stated in Psalm 81:10: *"Open your mouth wide, and I will fill it."* As the naba prophet begins to pray, his or her tongue is loosened, and prophecy begins to bubble up and flow. Often, a naba prophet will tell you where you came from, where you are, and where you are going. The message is heard and conveyed in the same breath, flowing like a river directly to the recipient, sometimes lasting for long periods of time.

Seer Prophets

A seer prophet is described as "an interpreter of oracles or of other hidden things; a foreteller; someone inspired by God to foretell or tell-forth (forth tell) the Word of God."[16] This type of prophet receives information primarily by *seeing*. Seer prophets can *see* any spirits, such as those of infirmity, witchcraft, fear, etc., on a person. These prophets are continually receptive to God.

The Old Testament words *roeh* (or *ra'ah*) and *chozeh* refer to two forms of the seer. The ra'ah[17] seer is an action visionary. That word comes from *mareh*—the act of sight, appearance, vision.[18] Ra'ah prophets see revelation in the form of external spiritual "action films." They are also gifted in interpretation.

Chozeh[19] seers receive still pictures in a more internal fashion as they close their eyes. They are not as keen as ra'ah prophets in the area of interpretation.

In Samuel's day, the *nabim* (naba) prophets began to have ecstatic experiences, and music became an important part of their prophesying (see

---

13. *Strong's* Hebrew reference 5012
14. *Strong's* Hebrew reference 5042
15. *Strong's* Hebrew reference 5016
16. *Strong's* Greek reference 4396
17. *Strong's* Hebrew reference 7203b
18. *Strong's* Hebrew reference 4758
19. *Strong's* Hebrew reference 2374

1 Chronicles 25:1), whereas the seers were "solitary, contemplative figures." Therefore, seers were labeled separately to distinguish between the two types.[20] As we read in 1 Samuel 9:9, *"Formerly in Israel, when a man went to inquire of God, he spoke thus: 'Come, let us go to the seer'; for he who is now called a prophet was formerly called a seer."*

Jeremiah Prophets

The Jeremiah prophet is often called the weeping prophet. These prophets grieve over the condition of the people they minister to, and cry out to God on their behalf. It is from this stream of prophets that proceed prophetic intercessors, evangelists, and missionaries. The utmost desire of Jeremiah prophets is to see souls enter the kingdom and nations repent, and their gifting promotes the fulfillment of this desire.

Modern-Day Examples of Specialized Prophets

I've had the privilege of meeting and training with some very noteworthy modern-day prophets. The following summaries of some I've known personally should give you a better understanding of the different types of prophets found in the world today.

Keep in mind that we shouldn't try to be "just like" like any other prophet, for God has designed us all differently. By all means, receive from other prophets, and honor them; but you must discover who God made you to be—*your* specialty—and then fulfill *your* purpose, call, and destiny. Your specialty may be unlike anyone we've known so far.

Let the Holy Spirit be your Elijah. It's great to have others lay hands on you, but more important is having an up-close and personal, intimate impartation from the Lord for yourself.

Mike Bickle of IHOP (International House of Prayer), in Grandview, Missouri, is primarily a Jeremiah prophet who focuses on prophetic intercession and aims to restore the worship and intercession components of the tabernacle of David internationally. I was blessed to be in the "first load" of

---

20. https://hermeneutics.stackexchange.com/questions/7887/why-is-a-seer-called-a-prophet (accessed June 8, 2018).

year one with him and the IHOP crew, in 1999-2000. God has used Mike to speak into my life at strategic times over the years.

WE SHOULDN'T TRY TO BE "JUST LIKE" LIKE ANY OTHER PROPHET, FOR GOD HAS DESIGNED US ALL DIFFERENTLY. BY ALL MEANS, RECEIVE FROM OTHER PROPHETS, AND HONOR THEM; BUT YOU MUST DISCOVER WHO GOD MADE YOU TO BE—*YOUR* SPECIALTY—AND THEN FULFILL *YOUR* PURPOSE, CALL, AND DESTINY.

Paul Cain has received many in-depth personal prophetic words for international Christian leaders and for those in government. The Lord would give him their private phone numbers, and he would call to speak to them. The government launched an investigation to find out how he had obtained top-secret government numbers. I was blessed to be in his Shiloh retreat in Kansas City, and he spoke five things over me that no one knew but God and me.

Kim Clement, now deceased, had an amazing gift of receiving accurate prophetic words for governments worldwide while in worship/intercession. He played piano and sang the words he would give. He is best known for prophesying that Donald Trump would become the forty-fifth president of the United States.

Bobby Conner, out of Bullard, Texas, is one of the most requested itinerant prophets alive today. He and his wife are longtime friends of mine. Bobby is accurate and has great integrity, travels extensively throughout the year, and has spoken to many serving in government.

Chuck Flynn, now deceased, had amazing apostolic/prophetic insight to help discover and raise up others who were called to ministry, myself included. God used him to speak into my life in 1989 and gave me an accurate outline of what God had called me to do. I thought Chuck was crazy when he said this to me, but everything he prophesied has come to pass in my life. Many people have been called into ministry via Chuck's prophetic voice.

James Goll and his late wife, Michal Ann, authored many books on prophecy, intercession, dreams, interpretation, compassion ministry, women in ministry, and prayer. Prophet Bob Jones has called James's book *The Seer* the best one ever written on the topic. Now living in Franklin, Tennessee, James continues to minister and raise up others across the nations. He and Michal Ann developed a yearly women's conference that many attend. I received an ordination from them and am a member of their Encounters Fellowship of Ministries.

Bishop Bill Hamon, of Christian International Ministries in Santa Rosa Beach, Florida, is considered the father of modern-day personal prophetic ministry. He has taught and activated thousands over the years to hear and convey the voice of God to individuals in the form of personal prophetic words. His main thrust is in teaching naba word prophesying. He has an incredible set of books that belong in the library of every prophetic person. His training changed my life, and my first ordination was under his ministry.

John Paul Jackson, now deceased, had a ministry that primarily focused on dreams and interpretation. He published a tremendous collection of books and videos on the topic—it is probably among the best resources on the subject.

Prophet Bob Jones, now deceased, was a seer of seers. He received many dreams and could tell you your own dream and its interpretation before you even shared it with him. As a true spiritual father to many, including myself, he held weekly mentoring meetings in his home. I attended his meetings for five years, and he trained me in the seer realm. Bob faithfully wrote down what the Lord showed him, even in the middle of the night. He had his spiral-bound notebook within reach at all times.

Rick Joyner is the founder of MorningStar Ministries in Fort Mill, South Carolina. He mainly ministers as a prophet to government and world leaders, covering signs of the times, historical data, and future events. He has a church, a fellowship of churches, and a school of ministry. He is also an incredible writer and teaches writing seminars. MorningStar also trains teams in personal prophetic ministry, and utilizes them to minister to conference attendees. As Rick's first secretary and office manager in 1990, I have been a part of MorningStar since the beginning. I have been ordained by his fellowship of ministries and am also a member of the local church. I'm thankful for Rick's input into my life over the years.

Steve Shultz is the founder of The Elijah List, today's foremost prophetic publication on the Internet. God uses Steve to keep the church informed of present-day prophets and their prophecies. Steve authors prophetic articles and books, and holds many prophetic conferences.

Lance Wallnau is mainly a prophet to the business world. However, he's recently taken a front-row seat to prophecy regarding government. He ministered with his friend Kim Clement, and they both prophesied that Donald Trump would become the forty-fifth president of the United States. Lance is famous for his Seven Mountains teaching, as well as for being a leader to those called into marketplace ministry.

David Wilkerson, now deceased, was primarily a prophetic evangelist. He filled his Times Square Church in New York City with saved drug addicts, prostitutes, and gangs. The book he wrote about it, *The Cross and the Switchblade*, was made into a movie. The Lord used him to accurately foretell the days yet to come in the book *Set the Trumpet to Thy Mouth*. I've been blessed to minister at his World Challenge ministry headquarters in Lindale, Texas.

Prophets of Doom

Jesus warned in Matthew 24:24, *"False christs and false prophets will rise and show great signs and wonders to deceive, if possible, even the elect."*

True to what He said, we have seen many false prophets arise as prophets of doom. Sadly, fake news fills the Internet. The sensationalists use scare tactics to pull people into their web for fame and fortune. We must have discernment and test the spirits, as God's Word directs us in 1 John 4:1.

At least once a year, someone claims to know the exact date of Jesus's return. The Bible is clear that no one knows the day or hour, not even Jesus or the angels. (See Matthew 24:36.)

ONE CLEAR WAY TO TEST IF A WORD OF JUDGMENT IS FROM THE LORD IS THAT GOD ALWAYS GIVES AN OPPORTUNITY TO REPENT, SO THAT THE JUDGMENT MAY BE CANCELED.

One clear way to test if a word of judgment is from the Lord is that God always gives an opportunity to repent, so that the judgment may be canceled. (See 2 Chronicles 7:14.)

God is love. He didn't create us so that He could destroy us. Every time a nation has repented, He restored it to a better position than it had before.

School of the Prophets

During the five years that I was blessed to be mentored by Prophet Bob Jones in his weekly home group, one thing became clear: A true prophet is not in it for himself. He takes seriously his job as a kingdom equipper.

As a true spiritual father to many, Bob made each feel as if we were his favorite. He told those he mentored that it saddened him to know not many other prophets were fathers. He emphasized that he would share with us only if we promised to share with others. He held nothing back in his "school of prophets."

We read of a school of prophets in the Old Testament. First Samuel 10:1–13 recounts what happened to Samuel when God sent him to be with the prophets. It changed him, and he "became another man," prophesying with them. (See 1 Samuel 10:6.) That is what happens to us in the midst of a group of prophets or prophetic people. The spirit of prophecy hovers over the group like a dove, and anyone who desires to prophesy may do so. It is like catching a wave in spiritual realms.

Prophetic conferences are a modern-day way of empowering those in attendance to enter a higher realm than any in which they have previously walked, rendering them changed forever.

Bishop Bill Hamon and his ministry, Christian International, are experts with their prophetic training and equipping program. They not only teach but also activate attendees in personal prophetic ministry. Taking that extra step into activation is crucial. They have developed many ways to help their students practice and apply what they have learned. Attendees are challenged and changed into prophesying machines.

Rick Joyner, with the prophetic conferences put on by MorningStar Ministries, offers a rare blend of training in worship, government, the arts, and prophecy. He has also developed a business network where marketplace ministers discuss and improve in their particular area of expertise.

The specialty of a ministry's head prophet is passed down to those who attend these conferences, and impartation happens.

Empowering Prophetic Women

The Lord led me to develop a series of conferences called Women's Prophetic Destiny, specifically designed to train and equip women to operate in the prophetic. We do three days of intense teaching and activation, as well as provide personal prophetic ministry and dream interpretation.

Today's women are no longer hiding inside their prayer closets. While personal, private prayer is an important practice for all believers, it is not the totality of what we are called to do. Therefore, we train and activate women in personal prophetic ministry, worship, interpretive dance, marketplace ministry, dream interpretation, evangelism, harp-and-bowl intercession, writing, homeschooling, counseling, parenting, deliverance, and the Israel mandate, just to name a few.

Prophetic Portals

In certain parts of the country are prophetic portals—specific areas where one may experience an open heaven and hear God to a greater degree than elsewhere. One example is Moravian Falls, North Carolina, where—for whatever reason—many people have reported experiencing angelic visitations. It's also a place where writers seem to flourish. Rick Joyner and MorningStar Ministries have offices and a retreat center there.

Don't be discouraged if you are unable to attend a specific conference or to visit a prophetic portal. God will meet you wherever you are. But no man is an island; we all need each other. Even if you can't attend a conference or go where there's a portal, I encourage you to reach out to others of like mind and heart around you. Consider starting your own prophetic group right in your home, in which you and your group may learn together, following the example of the apostle Paul:

> *Paul dwelt two whole years in his own rented house, and received all who came to him, preaching the kingdom of God and teaching the things which concern the Lord Jesus Christ with all confidence, no one forbidding him.* (Acts 28:30–31)

PRAYER

Dear Lord, help us to honor and learn from those who have gone before us, even as we seek to be who we are called to be. May we be those who will train and equip others and cause the kingdom to advance to Your glory. In Jesus's name, amen.

10

PROPHETIC INTERCESSION

Do you sometimes sense that something is "up," but you aren't quite sure what it is? You may spiritually sense that there is danger or sorrow ahead, and you may experience actual weeping—what I call "the weeping of the Holy Spirit." The purpose of this chapter is to help you recognize and work with the Holy Spirit when this happens.

Before we continue, please note that the contents of this chapter are intended for those with a prophetic gifting who are of stable mind. It is not meant to take the place of a mental health counselor or family physician whose input would be valuable to those whose emotional needs require professional help.

The Weeping of the Holy Spirit

Many prophetic intercessors have asked for help in understanding the weeping of the Holy Spirit. Even to those who know their tears are from the Lord, the experience can prove frightening. Yet there's no need to fear. The weeping of the Holy Spirit is a divine prompting to pray and thereby help thwart a tragic event or at least lessen its severity.

It may feel like depression or "the blues" creeping in. Women may brush it off as hormones. If you are a mentally healthy person, and everything else in your life is okay, then this sense of despair is not for yourself. You are spiritually standing in the gap for someone else's issue, be it of personal, corporate, national, or global import. A family member may be in danger, or it may be that a natural disaster or global catastrophe looms ahead. But there's good news: God has given to us the power to overcome, as well as the road map to victory.

What Does This Weeping Say to Us?

Read what the prophet Jeremiah wrote in Jeremiah 4:19:

O my soul, my soul! I am pained in my very heart! My heart makes a noise in me; I cannot hold my peace, because you have heard, O my soul, the sound of the trumpet, the alarm of war.

The enemy of our souls is out to kill, steal, and destroy (see John 10:10), but the Holy Spirit within us sounds the alarm and calls us to a winning battle. However, we must remember that *"the weapons of our warfare are not carnal but mighty through God for pulling down strongholds"* (2 Corinthians 10:4).

What Should We Do with This Weeping?

Let's give the Holy Spirit the "right-of-way," allowing Him to take over and direct our intercession. We must turn *to* it, not from it. *"Today, if you will hear His voice, do not harden your hearts"* (Hebrews 3:7–8).

God has given us a "G-force" (God-force) weapon called *praying in the Spirit*, also known as *praying in tongues*. Through this practice, we have the ability to pray, victoriously, that which the Spirit wants us to pray. As we do, He directs us with His own language so that we don't have to worry about what we should be praying.

The apostle Paul explained it well in his epistle to the Romans:

The Spirit also helps in our weaknesses. For we do not know what we should pray for as we ought, but the Spirit Himself makes intercession for us with groanings which cannot be uttered. Now He who searches the hearts knows what the mind of the Spirit is, because He makes intercession for the saints according to the will of God. And we know that all things work together for good to those who love God, to those who are the called according to His purpose. (Romans 8:26–28)

As we allow the weeping unction of the Holy Spirit to cry out within and through us, we pray…

1. past our own weaknesses for the root issues of which we do not have any personal knowledge (see verse 26).

2. in the will of God for specific situations (see verse 27).

3. for the things over which the Spirit within us is weeping (see verse 26).

4. in the way the Lord wants the prayer to be prayed (see verse 27).

5. in the will of the Lord (see verse 27).

6. for the outcome (see verse 28).

If we know that we pray according to God's will, we know that God hears us. First John 5:14 says, *"Now this is the confidence that we have in Him, that if we ask anything according to His will, He hears us."*

That's important. If we know He hears us, we can be sure of obtaining what we're asking for: *"And if we know that He hears us, whatever we ask, we know that we have the petitions that we have asked of Him"* (1 John 5:15).

Because God hears us, and because we pray according to His will, Romans 8:28 tells us that we have victory: *"And we know that all things work together for good to those who love God, to those who are the called according to His purpose."*

Additional Benefits of Praying in the Spirit

In addition, as we pray in the Spirit, we accomplish a host of other good things outlined in Jude 1:20–23:

> But you, beloved, building yourselves up on your most holy faith, **praying in the Holy Spirit**, keep yourselves in the love of God, looking for the mercy of our Lord Jesus Christ unto eternal life. And on some have compassion, making a distinction; but others save with fear, pulling them out of the fire, hating even the garment defiled by the flesh.

The above passage assures us that when we pray in the Spirit, we…

1. build ourselves up in faith on the inside (see verse 20).

2. keep ourselves in the love of God (see verse 21).

3. help ourselves to look for mercy (see verse 21).

4. walk in compassion (see verse 22).

5. have discernment (see verse 22).

6. have the fear of the Lord (see verse 23).

7. save others from destruction (see verse 23).

8. have successful evangelism (see verse 23).

9. hate defilement/desire holiness (see verse 23).

Pray Through Until the Release Occurs

One important benefit of praying in the Spirit (praying in tongues) is that it is a language the devil and his demons cannot understand. Therefore, they cannot thwart the outcome.

When praying in the Spirit, we may experience tears and/or groaning. Certainly, we do not have to make a show by doing it publicly. We can pray all alone in our prayer closet. Then, as we pray in secret, God will reward us openly. (See Matthew 6:6.)

We don't need to be afraid to allow the Holy Spirit to lead us when He causes His unction to come. It is a time to let the "rain" of the Holy Spirit "reign"—to let Him cry in and through us for souls and for mercy.

WE DON'T NEED TO BE AFRAID TO ALLOW
THE HOLY SPIRIT TO LEAD US WHEN HE
CAUSES HIS UNCTION TO COME.
IT IS A TIME TO LET THE "RAIN" OF THE HOLY
SPIRIT "REIGN"—TO LET HIM CRY IN AND
THROUGH US FOR SOULS AND FOR MERCY.

When those tears and/or deep groanings come, grab your Kleenex and just go with it until you feel a release. That is called "praying it through." Be balanced, and don't panic or pressure yourself.

Even if you don't have a prayer language of your own, you can still pray in the Spirit. In whatever way you do pray, continue doing so until you feel that release or a sense of peace.

Examples of Prophetic Intercession

Prophetic intercession can occur in other ways, as well.

Sometimes, the Lord will give us a dream or a flash vision of a person or a tragedy. We may randomly sense the need to pray for a specific person the Lord lays on our hearts. If this should happen, stop and ask the Lord what He wants to be done. Write it out, pray over it, and consider contacting the person the vision concerns, to be sure he or she is okay.

You may experience dreams, visions, feelings of apprehension, and other sensings. As you prophetically recognize what is happening, begin to war in the spirit accordingly.

Let me give you a few examples of some ways the Lord has spoken to me to intercede.

The Baby Dream

The Vietnam War left many Vietnamese babies orphaned and homeless. The United States decided to airlift planeloads of these orphans to America for adoption.

I was seventeen at the time, and, one night, I had a dream that I was in Vietnam, and one of the planes full of babies crashed on the runway. I hurriedly ran to and from the aircraft, getting the babies to safety and hollering directions to other people to help.

Little did I know, I was screaming aloud in my sleep. My sister woke me. I had been standing in the middle of my bedroom, screaming and directing traffic. As I dreamed I was really doing it.

I could no longer sleep. I cried and prayed about the dream all night. At daybreak, I went downstairs and turned on the television. The exact scene from my dream unfolded on the news.

To this day, I do not know if it was merely prophetic prayer intercession, or if I was literally translated there to help.

Babylon Experience

My son was a prodigal for some time. One night, he told me he was going to a friend's house to watch a movie. I didn't hear from him again; he wouldn't answer his cell phone. When I finally received a call from the friend's parents, we all concluded the boys were up to no good.

While I paced the floor in prayer, the Lord dropped this message into my spirit: "Pray that the vessels don't return to Babylon." I recognized the allusion to Jeremiah 27:18, and I thought about the Babylonian culture—drinking, partying, bad women.

I began to pray as the Lord had directed me: "If the boys are doing the right thing, I pray they have a great time. But if they are drinking alcohol, may it make them throw up. If they take any drugs, keep them safe; but I hope they have a trip that terrifies them.

"If they are messing around with bad girls, I hope they turn ugly right before their eyes. I pray they will hate Babylon so much, they will never want to return."

Hours later, my son called, wanting to know how to contact our auto service because he had a flat tire. It took a couple hours before help arrived.

He was in a foul mood when he finally got home. I wasn't, because I knew God had heard and answered my prayer. My son said, "What are you smiling about? I bet you prayed we would have a bad night." I replied, "I prayed that if you were doing the right thing, you'd have the best night of your life. So, it was your choice what type of night you ended up with."

I asked him for his car keys, as my own vehicle was in the shop at the time. Later, when I went outside to run an errand in his car, I leaned down to pull the driver seat forward, and that's when I saw something on the floor—a wristband from a nightclub. In big, bold letters, it read, "BABYLON." No wonder the Lord had said to pray that the vessels wouldn't return to Babylon! That was the name of the place where they'd gone. I still carry the wristband in my Bible to this day.

Notice how the Lord prophetically led me to pray and intercede through (1) a sensing in my spirit, (2) a little natural knowledge, and (3) the use of a Scripture verse.

Grandma Event #1

I woke up one morning from a dream about my daughter. In it, the Lord showed me she was pregnant. I knew she was on birth control. The Lord reminded me of the time I'd gotten pregnant while on birth control and had lost the baby. He told me to call her and tell her about the dream, and then to ask her to get checked so she wouldn't lose the baby.

She thought I was nuts. So, I just started praying for the baby's safety.

Later that day, a friend of mine and I were at a shopping mall, walking around on the second floor above a little playground on the first level. I clearly heard a little boy's voice shouting to me, "Gramma! Gramma!" But there was no sign of a little boy. I started to cry. "I'm going to be a grandmother to a little boy!" I told my friend, then went on to relate the rest of the story.

Over the next several days, I prayed continuously for the safety of my grandson.

A week or so later, my daughter came for Thanksgiving and informed me she was indeed pregnant. She'd had bronchitis, and the doctor had given her an antibiotic that, combined with the birth control pill she was on, had had the effect of a fertility drug. That's how my grandson, Zachary (his name means "remembrance of the Lord"), came to be.

The Lord had led me prophetically through a dream, connecting it with a natural, personal incident, and the prophetic experience of a little boy's voice calling to me. I interceded for the protection of my grandbaby, and God kept him safe.

Grandma Event #2

A couple of years later, I dreamed about an adorable little girl crawling up onto my lap, loving on me, and calling me "Gramma." She played with my mustard-seed necklace, which I wear as a sign of my faith.

Sure enough, my Megan came along. She is such a gift! And guess what? She has my middle name, Faith, which was represented by the mustard-seed necklace in my dream. Megan Faith is smart and beautiful, and she loves the Lord.

In this situation, the Lord spoke through a dream to tell me about my future granddaughter, as well as through the necklace to give me her middle name. I prayed, and baby Megan Faith came forth safely.

Grandma Event #3

Several years later, when both her kids were in grade school, my daughter enrolled in nursing school. I dreamed that she had a happy, healthy, smiling baby girl. In the dream, she and her husband were discussing whether Michelle (which means "God's messenger") should be the baby's first or middle name.

I told my daughter about my dream, and she said, "Mother, I'm busy in nursing school, and I'm on birth control. I'm not pregnant, nor am I going to get pregnant!" Well…it turns out she was wrong about that!

She had a rough pregnancy, and her doctors warned her of the possibility of the baby's being born with Down syndrome, heart problems, or deafness. I cried out to God, and He said, "Was the baby I showed you like that?" Of course, my answer was, "No." So, I began to refuse the other reports and started speaking in confident faith that Brooke Michelle would be just fine.

When Jennifer went in to have the baby, her mother-in-law and I remained together in the waiting room.

I suddenly had a bad feeling something was wrong, and I tried to call Jennifer's phone. For some reason, my phone dialed 9-1-1, instead. I tried Jennifer again. But every time I pressed the button for Jennifer's number, 9-1-1 came up. Those three digits had replaced Jennifer's number in my phone's contacts list. I quickly called three close friends and asked them to pray, and I started praying in tongues.

I finally tired of waiting and went back to the delivery room. Just then, the doctor greeted me and said, "Mother and baby are both fine."

I later found out that a nurse had accidently shot the epidural into the wrong spot in my daughter's spine, which had almost caused her to pass out in the midst of labor. That was the 9-1-1 issue. Brooke had a small hole in her heart that healed within six months. Everything else about her was perfect.

In this event, the Lord spoke through a dream about my daughter's pregnancy, as well as about the good health of the baby, so we would have that information to use as we "warred" against the evil projections. God gave me Brooke's middle name to reassure me that she would be a little messenger. And He used my phone and the 9-1-1 incident to help me war against what happened to my daughter during labor and delivery.

God used all these things to prophetically direct my intercessory efforts.

September 11, 2001

In the months before the September 11, 2001, attacks on the Twin Towers in New York City, many people experienced prophetic warnings. For some people I know, it seemed that they "happened" to look at their digital clocks whenever the time read 9:11, and this bothered them. After all, 9-1-1 is the number to call in case of an emergency. I told them to pray in the Spirit.

Not long before 9/11, I was having car trouble, so I had to take a Greyhound bus from Charlotte, North Carolina, to Frederick, Maryland, to do a meeting. As we drove across the George Washington Bridge in D.C., I saw a missile or a plane shoot across the road toward the Capitol, and I screamed. When I realized it was a vision, I apologized, telling the other folks on the bus that I must have had a bad dream. That night, when I spoke at the meeting, I charged the intercessors there to keep the vision in prayer as the gatekeepers of that region.

The Friday before the event occurred, my son had a dream that he described to me as "our country under attack." He lived in a different city and felt compelled to come home quickly to be together with the rest of our family. He sensed something bad would happen soon. As we watched the attacks unfold on television, and he saw the first tower coming down, he said, "Just one was hit? The other one is going to be hit, too—right here!" As he pointed, the second plane hit the second tower in the exact spot he indicated. He then said he'd dreamed that other planes were going to strike in other places, so we called others on the phone and asked them to intercede along with us.

What occurred on 9/11 was terrible, but I believe the intercession of many helped to prevent even more tragedies from occurring.

Trouble on the Horizon

When you have an ominous sense, a panicky feeling, or a bad dream, you aren't crazy; you are probably receiving a directive from the Holy Spirit to participate in prophetic intercession. Pray what you feel led to pray in the natural, then pray in the Spirit for the rest. God will use you mightily, and your prayers *will* make a difference.

Sometimes, people sense or dream of accidents, illnesses, or deaths. Do not allow yourself to accept that any tragic event is unstoppable. God gives us a prophetic "sneak peek" at the enemy's plans so that we may pray against them. Sometimes, our intercession will lessen the scope of a tragedy; other times, it will prevent it from occurring at all. So, pray!

PRAYER

Dear Lord, please help us to recognize and rightly respond when Your Holy Spirit calls us to intercede. Use us to help cancel the plans of the enemy and protect those in harm's way. In Jesus's name, amen.

11

WRITING PROPHETIC ARTICLES

It is important to keep track of what the Lord has spoken to us. Jeremiah 30:2 says, *"Thus speaks the LORD God of Israel, saying: 'Write in a book for yourself all the words that I have spoken to you.'"* The prophet Samuel didn't allow a single word the Lord spoke to him fall to the ground. (See 1 Samuel 3:19.)

Many times, we dream or receive a thought from the Lord, only to have it disappear after a few moments. That's why it's important to capture and preserve those fleeting thoughts or messages. You may choose to record yourself summarizing the vision on either the voice recorder on your phone or a digital recorder, or perhaps you'll do it the old-fashioned way and write it down, always keeping a pen and paper handy.

YOU MAY BE SURPRISED BY THE WAY THAT SOME OF YOUR SEEMINGLY SMALL, FLEETING THOUGHTS WILL TURN OUT TO BE PROPHETIC MESSAGES THAT THE LORD WILL EXPOUND UPON LATER. SUCH AN EXPERIENCE IS BOUND TO ENCOURAGE YOU, AND IT JUST MAY TOUCH SOMEONE ELSE'S HEART.

You may be surprised by the way that some of your seemingly small, fleeting thoughts will turn out to be prophetic messages that the Lord will expound upon later. Such an experience is bound to encourage you, and it just may touch someone else's heart. Quite often, many of us face similar challenges at the same time, as though the enemy is launching a widespread attack. When you write about your experience, recording how God came through for you, others facing similar circumstances will be encouraged and blessed.

It was more than thirty years ago that I began the practice of writing down whatever the Lord spoke to me. At the encouragement of a friend, I developed an e-mail list in the late 1990s, and I would send those writings, in the form of articles, to my close friends, the members of my ministry covering, and anyone else who was interested in receiving them. The more I traveled in ministry, the more the recipient list grew. Little did I know, God was helping me to develop chapters for future books.

Because I travel so frequently, it is often difficult or even impossible to write down everything the Lord gives me. So, I purchased a small digital recorder, which I use to record myself relating that which I will eventually type up. As an affirmation of this practice, the Lord gave me this Scripture: *"My heart is overflowing with a good theme; I recite my composition concerning the King; **my tongue is the pen of a ready writer**"* (Psalm 45:1).

It is amazing to see how much can flow from a tiny thought once we begin to speak it aloud. God tells us that if we will open our mouths, He will fill them. (See Psalm 81:10.) As He does, we will fill a blog or even a future book.

There is a voice-recognition software called Dragon Naturally Speaking that helps you write as you speak, making your tongue truly to be the pen of a ready writer. It is a special application that you talk into, and it writes what you say. It takes a while to train it to transcribe your voice, but it *does* work. You can purchase the software online, as a download, or at certain stores. It isn't totally accurate, so you must be sure to proofread the transcriptions!

If you have an iPhone, your "Notes" application will do the same thing. I use my iPhone to record ministry notes to as I travel and speak. These notes eventually become articles for my newsletter.

Quite often, I come across people who say they can teach a roomful of people, but they find it nearly impossible to write. Handed a pen or a computer keyboard, they find their minds going blank. For many such people, a digital recorder or voice-recognition software is the answer. Many ministers hire transcribers to type the recordings of their teachings for the same reason.

The naba word—proceeding word from the mouth of God—happens as we minister but not necessarily while we're merely writing. Thus, as we speak from our notes, God breaks in and adds material that isn't on the page. If we haven't been recording our meeting, we are likely to forget exactly what we said. That's why I encourage those I mentor to record every part of *all* their meetings.

Writing Articles

If you are just starting out with writing for an audience, I recommend starting with articles. God may have a book—or even several books—inside you, but it's best to hone your writing skills by working first on shorter compositions as you develop the discipline necessary for authoring books.

You may want to collect your articles and compile them each year in the form of a short book. In many cases, the messages are timeless.

Don't wait until you "feel like" writing. If you sit down and devote the time to write, the Holy Spirit will show up. When you speak to Him, He speaks to you.

Doing Research

We can't afford to harbor a religious spirit about our writing. It could be that God wants us to know further information than is conveyed within one Holy-Spirit download. Many times, He gives us just enough to whet our appetite to research and discover more. As we pursue the things He prompts us toward, He will release additional facts regarding the topic, and a more profound written message will develop as a result.

Every year, I do a great deal of research at the times of Rosh Hashanah and Yom Kippur (the Jewish New Year). The Lord often speaks through numbers, so the number of the Jewish New Year is important. I like to study what is represented by the numerals of a particular year, and the article I write starts to grow as the Lord reveals more of what is projected for the New Year.

At times, an article flows from beginning to end, and I send it out right away. But, at other times, I regret sending an article so quickly because I end up receiving additional, pertinent information by the next morning. Some prophetic messages have a time stamp and should be dispersed right away. With other messages, it's important to hold on to them until they are complete.

Telling Your Story

If the Lord lays a particular topic on your heart, research the topic, and then speak or write from your heart about what you find. The result may well be a prophetic message that will touch hearts and change lives.

You may receive a "wild" message that includes a lot of supernatural action you may want to convey as an allegory in order to minimize the risk of alienating your audience. Certain scenes, if presented without any filter, will invoke great criticism from the religious community. The important part is to get the message out in a form that will reach those whom God wants you to reach. Don't get offended about terminology. You know the difference between an actual spiritual experience and a figment of your own imagination.

Quit letting the enemy stop your writing gift with his excuses and attacks. Don't die with those things the Lord gave you tucked inside you. If you will write, then, when you leave this earth, those words can continue to speak on your behalf to future generations.

Film Writing

God is using the film industry to tell the story of our Lord. It may be that you have been called for such a time as this, to write a screenplay of such value to the kingdom that it will rival the books and movies the world has produced. You will never know unless you try.

Getting the Word Out

When you receive a prophetic word for the church or for our nation, don't keep it hidden in your notebook or on your computer. God doesn't give us these types of words for us to keep to ourselves. You might consider starting a blog or using social media. Whatever method you choose, be sure to keep a copy of your work saved to your computer and as a hard copy, as well.

Writing Books

A friend once told me, "Inch by inch is a cinch; yard by yard is too hard." That maxim certainly applies to the process of writing a book. Any task, done one step at a time, becomes less daunting.

Don't be afraid to research available information to help prepare you to write a book. Writing workshops, as well as many books on writing, can help. For myself, *Write to Ignite* by Deborah Joyner Johnson, *On Writing* by Stephen King, and *The Elements of Style* by William Strunk Jr. were particularly helpful materials. One of the most encouraging things I did was to attend the MorningStar Writer's Seminar. Gathering together with other aspiring authors to learn from experts of the craft is invaluable.

Don't be tempted to keep trying to redo your book while in the midst of writing it. First, finish the initial draft; only then should you go back through it and make revisions. Enlist people you trust to help you with the proofreading.

Most important of all, get an editor. They will not only proofread for spelling errors but will also make sure you have presented your content properly and with clarity. They will frustrate and challenge you, and will rid you of any pride in the process, but the result will be worth it.

Thou Shalt Not Steal

If you are quoting prophetic material from another minister, make sure you give proper credit. The Bible specifically warns about those who steal prophetic words He gives to someone else: "'Therefore behold, I am against the prophets,' says the LORD, 'who steal My words every one from his neighbor'" (Jeremiah 23:30).

Other people have stolen prophetic words from me. There was a man who would always ask me, "So, what's the Lord speaking to you lately?" I would answer him, and he would say, "That's exactly what He told me." The next thing I knew, he would use that prophecy at a conference or in an article he sent out on the Internet.

A lady minister did the same thing to me. One time, her rendition of my information became her most famous material. I had to forgive her and let it go. God promised me that if I did, He would give me much more, and He has.

For a while, I felt almost crazy over the whole infringement issue, becoming uncertain as to whether others had copied me or I had copied them. I asked God what to do. I felt Him telling me not to respond to any questions about what God was speaking to me until after I'd finished writing my own articles and had sent them out.

Remember that we serve an awesome God who is everywhere. Growing up, I learned from our church pastor about the *universality of the Holy Spirit*. God *can* speak the same thing to someone else on the other side of the planet from us. However, we know whether we have received a word from Him on our own or whether we have pirated it. Let's be honest and give credit to the one who deserves it if we use someone else's material.

Spread the Word

If you feel you have received prophetic insight that should reach a wider audience, forward it to the proper sources.

Several prophetic groups on the Internet accept material from others. The primary one is the Elijah List. You can submit material to them through their website.

One time, the Lord gave me an encouraging poem that I felt I was to send to as many sources as possible. I spent hours pulling up the e-mail addresses of news sources as well as those of major Christian Internet publishers. That week, I received e-mails from people around the country whose lives had been blessed as a result. God is faithful!

Find Your Writing Gift Style

The Lord gave me a dream in which we stood in His office in heaven. Many boxes had been delivered there and were stacked all around us. God grabbed several boxes and prepared to give them to me, as He wanted me to help distribute the contents. He first opened each box to explain the contents.

The boxes contained ink pens. Some boxes had pens of all the same color. Others had pens of a variety of colors. The colors defined the type of writing gift each pen represented when given to someone. Green signified teaching. Blue represented revelation. Pink signified passion for the Lord. Purple indicated royal authority. Gold represented His glory. There were other colors and corresponding meanings, as well.

God said, "I want these to be given to My aspiring authors and songwriters. I'll show you some of them as you travel. Tell them to be sure to use what I've given them, as what they write will break yokes of bondage off many people."

After that experience, He began to show me, in meetings as I traveled, specific people to whom that word related. I would then call them out and minister to them about it as He led me.

If you have a desire in your heart to write what the Lord speaks to you, God has placed it there. As you focus on hearing from the Lord, the more you use the gift, the better you will get. Just do it.

12

PROPHETIC WORSHIP

I was raised in my early childhood in the Baptist church, where we didn't raise our hands or do anything but sing along with the hymnal during our times of worship. When I was thirteen, my family started attending a rocking, Spirit-filled Pentecostal church, in which my understanding of worship began to expand.

In my twenties, I finally began to "get it." I'll never forget the first time I lifted my hands in worship. With my elbows tucked close to my sides, I managed to raise my forearms in front of me as if someone were holding me at gunpoint. I felt nervous and thought everyone was looking at me, but that wasn't the case. The rest of the people were even more into the worship than I was, so why would they have been watching what I did? The enemy likes to whisper his lies in an effort to stifle our worship, but, this time, I realized the truth.

Through the years, the Lord led me on a fascinating journey to discover just how powerful worship can be. It was as a young single mother that I learned worship itself is a major key in overcoming the trials we face.

For instance, I discovered that worship causes the Lord to show up. His Word tells us that He inhabits the praises of His people. (See Psalm 22:3 KJV.) *Inhabit* means "to occupy as a place of settled residence or habitat: live in; to be present in or occupy in any manner or form."

Once I allowed myself to become freed up in worship, I also became freed up in many other areas of my life. It is empowering when God comes and inhabits our praises.

Obviously, if we want to communicate with God and have a relationship with Him—if we desire for Him to show up and listen to us—we need to start praising Him. We must *"enter into His gates with thanksgiving, and into His courts with praise"* (Psalm 100:4). Once we've done that, the next step is going into the Holy of Holies. How exciting!

Restoration of the Tabernacle of David

The tabernacle of David is the only one God has promised to restore (see Acts 15:16), and part of that tabernacle includes spontaneous, ongoing praise and worship. In the Bible, we read about the Levites, God's skilled artisans in the tabernacle. Here is an overview of some of their functions:

> *And he stationed the Levites in the house of the LORD with cymbals, with stringed instruments, and with harps, according to the commandment of David, of Gad the king's seer, and of Nathan the prophet; for thus was the commandment of the LORD by His prophets. The Levites stood with the instruments of David, and the priests with the trumpets. Then Hezekiah commanded them to offer the burnt offering on the altar. And when the burnt offering began, the song of the LORD also began, with the trumpets and with the instruments of David king of Israel.* (2 Chronicles 29:25–27)

Prophetic Songs of the Lord

Prophetic songs of the Lord are powerful. Something about them invokes a tangible sensing of the presence of the Lord. They are spontaneous in nature and begin to flow as the anointing settles upon the vessel being used.

As prophecies are sung over people, the naba word proceeding from the mouth of God bubbles up and out of the psalmist in song to the recipient. Often, it comes in the form of a rhyme, which, as Prophet Bob Jones taught me, is a high level of the prophetic. It's hard enough being prophetic without having to make sure a word follows a specific rhyme scheme. When a word flows in rhyme without any effort on our part, we know the word is from the Lord.

Prophetic Songs of Deliverance

Sometimes, the act of singing prophetically over someone will turn into the singing of songs of deliverance—spontaneous prophetic songs with a deliverance anointing that sets captives free from spiritual bondages. As the song begins to flow, it is powerful, often breaking yokes that resisted years of counseling. These songs are solemn yet potent.

SOMETIMES, THE ACT OF SINGING PROPHETICALLY OVER SOMEONE WILL TURN INTO THE SINGING OF SONGS OF DELIVERANCE—SPONTANEOUS PROPHETIC SONGS WITH A DELIVERANCE ANOINTING THAT SETS CAPTIVES FREE FROM SPIRITUAL BONDAGES.

It's amazing to behold what God does in the services where prophetic songs of deliverance are employed. Often, simultaneous deliverances occur throughout the room, even when another person isn't singled out for ministry. This type of deliverance isn't one for which you can set an appointment. It occurs sovereignly, as the psalmist is led by the Holy Spirit.

Harp-and-Bowl Intercession

Prophetic songs of intercession are also known as "harp-and-bowl" intercession, meaning a combination of worship and intercession/prayer.

Harp-and-bowl intercession gets its name from a reference in the book of Revelation:

Now when He had taken the scroll, the four living creatures and the twenty-four elders fell down before the Lamb, each having a harp, and golden bowls full of incense, which are the prayers of the saints. And they sang a new song, saying.... (Revelation 5:8–9)

This type of intercession may involve a worship team playing spontaneous music; prophetic singers singing along with spontaneous prophetic songs, while others interject spoken prayers; and Scriptures being sung or spoken. All is prophetically led by the Lord. It often involves antiphonal singing, a style that works by call and response.

Warfare Worship Intercession

Warfare worship intercession usually occurs with warring drums setting the cadence. It takes on a sound similar to an army marching to war, because that's what is happening, only in the spiritual rather than the natural realm. It is spontaneous in nature and includes the declaration and proclamation of Scriptures. Warfare worship intercessors often use flags, boxing hand motions, kicks, stomps, and rods—broomstick-like tools carved with Scriptures and biblical symbols relating a person's testimony—with which they strike the floor. The use of a rod denotes defeating the enemy by the blood of the Lamb and the word of one's testimony. (See Revelation 12:11.)

Prophetic Interpretive Dance

Prophetic interpretive dance is led by the Holy Spirit and is sometimes accompanied by angels in the unseen realm. This activity can occur in conjunction with a prerecorded song or with live music; however, music is not necessary, as the dancing may occur without it. This type of dance tells a story or brings forth a message through liturgical moves. There may be just one dancer or a team of dancers, and the type of dance may be anything from ballet to jazz to modern dance, and so forth. The spontaneous leading of the Holy Spirit interprets His message through the art of dance.

Prophetic interpretive dance is not necessarily performed by professional dancers. If the participants are following the spontaneous leading of the Lord, the resulting art will be beautiful, regardless of their level of dance expertise.

Prophetic Skilled Artisans

Another form of prophetic worship is prophetic art made through charcoal drawings, painting, or simple sketches. Artists simply allow the Holy Spirit to lead and direct what they create during a worship service. Once the artwork is finished, one senses a particular theme or message spoken through the piece of art that was created.

Additional forms of prophetic art, such as pottery or jewelry, may also occur in this type of environment. The key is spontaneous creation led by the Holy Spirit that conveys some type of prophetic theme or message.

Worship Is Your War-Ship

At a New Year's service at my church one year, the Lord spoke to me, saying, "From now on, worship will be your war-ship." That pronouncement has stuck with me ever since. When I am going through trials, I know that if I can just make it to church in time for worship, things will be better.

Somehow, some way, worship seems to carry us to another level where we can sense victory even when we don't yet see it manifested. The Lord wars on our behalf as we worship Him.

God sent the praisers out ahead of the battle in 2 Chronicles 20, with the result that the enemy turned on themselves, prompting their own defeat. And God will do no less for us.

> "Thus says the LORD to you: 'Do not be afraid nor dismayed because of this great multitude, for the battle is not yours, but God's....You will not need to fight in this battle. Position yourselves, stand still and see the salvation of the LORD, who is with you, O Judah and Jerusalem!' Do not fear or be dismayed; tomorrow go out against them, for the LORD is with you."... Now when they began to sing and to praise, the LORD set ambushes against the people of Ammon, Moab, and Mount Seir, who had come against Judah; and they were defeated.
>
> (2 Chronicles 20:15, 17, 22)

It never ceases to amaze me when a speaker prefers to hide in a side room and stay there until it is time for him or her to speak. Worship is the most important part of any service, because worship is when *we* minister to *God*. He inhabits the praises of us, His people, and directs us so that we can be a blessing to His kingdom.

Don't miss out on your opportunity to honor God before you get up to speak. If you feel the need to pray more before you get up to minister, plan on arriving early and doing it before worship; or, "pray on the way," i.e., during worship. Alternatively, be prayed up before you go. But don't miss out on being "under the spout where the glory comes out." As our praises go up, God's glory comes down.

As we worship God, He joins us, and miraculous things occur in His presence. We don't have to wait for a designated time during a church service to worship the Lord. We can worship Him at home, in the woods, in our cars—anywhere!

Because God inhabits His praises, the creativity of the Lord flourishes when we worship Him. Inventions and answers are released. Bodies and minds are healed; lives are restored. He may release the direction we need personally or for a business venture.

DON'T LET THE ENEMY MAKE YOU CONSISTENTLY LATE FOR CHURCH SO THAT YOU MISS THE BEST PART OF SERVICE—THE PART WHERE WE WORSHIP AND DECLARE OUR LOVE FOR GOD. SOMETHING RESTORATIVE OCCURS DURING THAT TIME.

Don't let the enemy make you consistently late for church so that you miss the best part of service—the part where we worship and declare our love for God. Something restorative occurs during that time.

Worship acts like the dew of the earth. As our praises rise, God's miracles and blessings come down like rain and shower us with His love.

Progressive Worship

In the realms of prophetic worship, there is a freedom now being experienced and expressed as younger Christian musicians allow themselves to be swept into the realms of the Holy Spirit and convey a whole new arena of musical sounds and feelings. It touches areas previously forbidden by standard music protocols. It's called *progressive worship*.

Just as a naba prophetic word is progressive, so is this newly labeled area of progressive prophetic worship that is beginning to evolve. It goes beyond sound, into an experience of freedom in worship that the modern day church has rarely encountered. God inhabits His praises, and desires to instruct and lead us into divine encounters whenever He shows up.

This new wave in the area of prophetic worship often results in just that. The cloud of the Lord has shown up in services as a resulting sign of God's stamp on it.

The Israelites offered abandoned worship to a golden calf and grieved the heart of God. Only He deserves our free, abandoned worship. Our young people are attempting to capture and lead the way in this hour through this new genre of worship. To our young people, much of the church's organ playing hymns seem boring and religious. They have a deep-seated need to experience and express Him in a very real way.

Like anything, we must tread cautiously and keep our spiritual senses attuned to the Lord. We do not want to worship the act of worship, nor end up abandoning Him and getting caught up into otherworldly spiritual experiences that are not of Him.

Always allow God's Word to be the plumb line, and test the spirits to be sure what is done is of Him. Don't abandon common sense and His Word just to attempt something different, trying to avoid what we think is a religious spirit. In the process, that would simply mean that we have a religious spirit about not having a religious spirit. God forbid.

PRAYER

Dear Lord, thank You for restoring the tabernacle of David and harp-and-bowl worship to us. How awesome it is to get lost in worshipping You so that we may find the treasures of relationship with You. Please show us how to worship in the way that pleases You most. In Jesus's name, amen.

13

PROPHETIC WORKING OF MIRACLES

As a child, I *sort of* attended several Kathryn Kuhlman meetings at Melody Land Christian Center in Southern California. I never saw Kathryn Kuhlman in person, but I did hear her. With five kids in our family, my mother wouldn't let us go inside with her and my dad. So, we would sit outside in the car and listen. The experience was similar to watching a movie at a drive-in theater, only without a screen to watch. I remember the excitement of people who had gotten healed during Kathryn's meetings and how they wanted to learn how she'd done it. Fortunately for me, my mother was an exceptionally dramatic woman who was glad to reenact what she'd witnessed at home.

A few days after the meetings, my parents left me and two of my siblings in the car at a grocery store. I saw several people walk by who needed healing, so I stretched out my arm like my mother had said Kathryn Kuhlman had done, and I hollered, "Be healed, in the name of Jesus!" A man in a wheelchair just smiled and waved when he was pushed past our car. I mumbled, "Why doesn't he get out of that thing? I prayed for him, and he got healed!" My sister reminded me that I wasn't Kathryn Kuhlman, so he probably hadn't gotten healed.

I have always hated to see people in pain—whether physical, mental, or emotional—and my life's desire has been to see people healed.

Perfect Healing

When I grew older, I worked for a large church, and the pastor's aged father-in-law took ill. At our staff meeting, the pastor said that his father-in-law was requesting prayer. He followed up his comment with these words: "We have to remember that he's up in age now, so it just might be time for his perfect healing."

I raised my hand and asked, "When you say that, do you mean 'time for him to die'?"

"Yes, Joni," the pastor replied. "We'll all eventually die and obtain our perfect, new body."

I just couldn't let it go. "Pastor," I persisted, "where is the Scripture that says death is our perfect healing? I've looked, and I can't find it. Nowhere does it say, 'The multitudes came to Jesus, and He stretched forth His hand, and immediately they all fell *dead* into their *perfect healing*.' Nowhere! Can you see headlines of the *Jerusalem Times*? 'Jesus Arrives: Another Gathering of the Grateful Dead.' Are the cemeteries located beside churches a sign of their latest healing service?"

The elders collapsed into laughter, and the pastor stood there, stunned. "People, I believe we just heard prophetically from the Lord," he said. "Joni, lead us in prayer for my father-in-law."

The pastor's father-in-law recovered and was soon back teaching our Sunday school class.

Experiences in the Healing Ministry

I have been blessed to learn how to minister in healing alongside my good friend Steven Zarit of Share The Flame Ministry. Steven was general manager of Vineyard Ministries International for John Wimber and traveled with John throughout the world as he taught on healing and deliverance. Prophet Bob Jones has said that Steven has the most powerful healing anointing of anyone he's ever seen. Because of that, Steven has often suffered attacks on his own health. I have experienced instantaneous healing as Steven has prayed for me. I once asked him for some pointers on healing, and he agreed to share them, on the condition that I give him some pointers on the prophetic. Talk about a great deal!

Steven instructed me to first invite the Holy Spirit to come, and then to watch the face and eyes of those for whom I prayed. He said to watch for eyes fluttering, faces contorting, facial expressions indicating fear, or other spirits coming upon the people, as all of these things represent spiritual activity. He told me to ask those for whom I was praying to keep their eyes open during prayer in order for me to see what is "in there." After all, the eyes are the windows to the soul. (See Matthew 6:22–23.)

We also need to discern whether we ought to address what we see. One time, while praying for a young man, I saw two sets of eyes moving back and forth in his head. The other woman ministering with me saw the same thing. It was obvious this young man had several inhabitants, and both of us felt led to simply pray for peace and safety for the boy.

Because of my lack of training in deliverance at the time, I did not feel prepared to handle such an intense situation. I did give the boy's father the necessary information for him to make a decision to consult with someone better equipped to help him.

There is no patented formula for healing or deliverance, but I do believe healing and deliverance happen by our speaking the Word of God, praying, and following the leading of the Holy Spirit. The outcome is always up to God.

Brain-Tumor Miracle

I stayed at a beautiful bed-and-breakfast on Solomons Island in Maryland while ministering to a local women's chapter of Aglow International. After breakfast, I met on the porch with the ladies of their board. They drew my attention to a house on another point. They told me that the man who lived there was scheduled to undergo surgery for a brain tumor on Monday, and that he had asked if their speaker would pray for him. I said, "Sure!" and started walking toward the house. They grabbed my arm and said, "Not there. Here. He doesn't want any company."

I didn't voice my concern that he would die since he didn't want us to lay hands on him or anoint him with oil, as instructed in the Bible. But then the Lord reminded me about the story of the centurion whose servant Jesus healed from afar. (See Matthew 8:5–13.) So, I prayed along that vein, and we sent the word of healing. Suddenly, I had an open vision of the gentleman's tumor as the talon of a bird clutching his brain. Angry, I cursed the tumor and commanded it to shrivel up and die, so it would enable the doctors to insert a vacuum hose into the man's head and suck out the remains of the tumor.

The following Monday afternoon, I received a phone call from someone who was excited to report that the surgery had happened exactly as we had prayed it would. When the doctors had inserted a camera on a thin hose to see the location of the tumor, they saw that the tumor had shriveled up and died. Then they inserted a vacuum hose and sucked out the remains. They repeated the process to be sure they had removed every part. Two days later, they sent the gentleman home with only a couple of stitches.

Ministering to the Suicidal

At a meeting in Alabama, there was a young man who reminded me of another boy I knew. As I called him out, the Lord began to give me further details that were similar to the story of the boy I knew. God had me address a spirit of suicide and cancel its assignment. The Lord delivered the young man, who currently ministers to other young people struggling with suicidal thoughts.

Ministering to the Sexually Abused

In the charismatic church, it is not uncommon for people to be treated wrongly because of general exuberance. Most Christians like to hug one another, but it is important to use caution in situations where we are ministering to a victim of sexual abuse. Since we may not know in advance if that's the case, we should always ask permission before hugging someone.

While traveling, I attended a church where the leaders recognized me. They approached me in the congregation and asked me to help minister to a young lady. When I agreed, they led me to a side room, where I discovered I would be ministering to her with two men. I was asked to lead the session.

When the young woman came in with her mother, the Lord showed me that her own father had sexually abused her. The men started to reach out to touch her, so I gently stopped them and whispered, "I think we're supposed to do this without touching her."

I knew that the way we spoke to her would prove vital. Thus, I did not come right out and say that her father had sexually abused her. What I said went something like this: "The Lord deeply loves you, and His heart is grieved by some of what has happened to you. He knows and sees it all and is bringing healing and deliverance to you from what happened at the hands of a trusted family member."

Massive deliverance ensued. The two men with me picked up on and used the same mode of language. I know the girl to this day, and she is now happily married, has children, and is living a normal life.

The young woman has since said that the two men's treating her with respect and dignity played a big part in bringing forth her healing and deliverance that day.

Ministering to the Mentally Ill

We should be sensitive and avoid embarrassing anyone with specific details when praying for deliverance.

WE SHOULD BE SENSITIVE AND AVOID EMBARRASSING ANYONE WITH SPECIFIC DETAILS WHEN PRAYING FOR DELIVERANCE.

One time, as I ministered to a woman at a church, I saw a spirit of mental illness on her. I began to pray by sharing with her a scriptural truth: "God has not given you the spirit of fear, but of power, love, and a sound mind." (See 2 Timothy 1:7.) I then cautiously prayed against all the spirits I saw that were troubling her. I stressed God's love for her and spoke confidence in Him into her spirit. I ended with a prayer for her to have a good night's sleep, which was something I sensed she hadn't had in a long time.

A few days later, I ministered at another meeting in the area. The leaders brought a woman to me at the end, and she said, "You don't recognize me, do you?" I didn't. It turned out to be the same woman from the church, but she looked unrecognizably different. She said she had been in and out of thirteen mental institutions and hadn't had a decent night's sleep in many years. But there she stood, completely delivered and having had several nights of peaceful rest.

Miracle Healing in Arkansas

At a meeting in Fort Smith, Arkansas, a young couple approached me, and we began to talk. I noticed that the young man bent his neck downward. They stated he had been experiencing headaches that went down the neck and into the back, and they asked me to pray for him.

I recall thinking, *If he would use better posture, maybe his head, neck, and back wouldn't hurt.* (Thank goodness other people can't view our thoughts as speech bubbles!)

The young wife walked away to talk to someone she recognized, so I called another gentleman over to help. I prayed as I felt led, and at the end of the prayer, I had a flash vision in which the Lord said, "Tell the man to roll his shoulders back like this," and demonstrated. I obeyed. When the man followed my instructions, his neck made a loud cracking noise, and the man stood upright with an astonished look on his face. "The pain is gone!" he exclaimed.

Immediately, his wife ran to him, screaming, "It's gone! Oh, my God! It's gone! His hump is gone! He's been a humpback all his life! The hump is gone!"

What did I know? I'd thought he just had bad posture. Nevertheless, God used me as I followed His directives.

A Self-Healing Dream

My back once gave me problems, and I blamed it on my frequent travel at the time. One time in particular, I knew I was suffering a pinched sciatic nerve. I felt miserable but had several more meetings to do before I could return home and visit my chiropractor.

That night as I slept, I had a dream. The Lord told me to lie on my left side, to extend my left leg straight, and to bend my right leg. Then, I was to use my hand to push my right hip forward as I turned my upper body in the opposite direction.

All of a sudden, I awakened to a large cracking noise and a sensation of sharp pain. I realized I had followed the instructions in my sleep. My hip was back in place, and my sciatic nerve was no longer pinched.

The Knee

In the early days of the now-famous Toronto Outpouring, a man known as one of the catalysts of the movement came to the Charlotte area and asked local churches for volunteers to assist with the crowds. I had twisted my right knee and was in pain, but I went anyhow. When he called for a healing line, I entered it, hoping to get some relief.

The minister said someone had a problem with their *left* knee, but it sounded exactly like the situation with my *right* knee.

I said, "That's me, but it's my right knee."

"No, this is a left knee," he replied. "Let me take care of this first."

For almost an hour, he went around trying to find the person needing healing in the left knee. I continued reminding him about my right knee, but he kept saying, "No! It's a *left* knee."

Finally, he stopped in front of me and seemed to be thinking out loud as he said, "I know it's the left knee, but I get this word every time I'm in front of you. What's going on?"

I looked at his left knee and noticed it was directly across from my own, painful right knee. I then asked, "Could it be because your left knee is across from my right knee?"

The light of revelation struck his face. "Oh, my goodness! I'm so sorry!" he exclaimed, then dropped to his knees and prayed for my right knee, and I was healed.

That experience was as an eye-opener for me, teaching me to use caution about asking if God wants to heal a specific body part (right or left, etc.). He wants both sides of our bodies to be well.

Raising the Dead

We hear a lot about miracles of the dead raising to life again in foreign nations, but this miraculous event happens here in the United States, too. The following are some miraculous situations I have personally experienced.

My mother battled many health problems throughout her life. She suffered heart attacks starting in her thirties and strokes in her later years. She was often near death. I prayed for healing and life for her each time she faced another health issue. Until the end of her life, I didn't fully know what had taken place at those times.

Because of strokes in her latter days, she could not speak well, but I still understood what she tried to communicate.

My dad and older brother brought her to my home one evening, and she shooed them out of the room so she could speak to me in private. She got down on her knees in front of me and begged for me to pray that she would die.

I was shocked. I told her I couldn't do that, and then I asked why she would request such a thing. She let me know that every time she nearly died, she had been sent back because I had prayed for her to live. She wanted me to quit doing that and instead to pray for her to die.

I told her that I would never pray for her to die but said I could let her go the next time if I was certain she had come to salvation. She said she wasn't sure if she was saved, and I had the honor of leading her back to God.

She then removed the framed photos of various family members from my wall, letting me know her remorse over having abused each one by acting things out with his or her picture. I promised I would explain to my dad so he could help her go to each one and apologize. I also let her know that I forgave her for the physical and verbal abuse she had inflicted on me.

Soon after, she had my dad take her to see every family member to repent and seek forgiveness. Two weeks later, she passed away. I kept my promise and let her go.

It amazed me to know I'd actually raised her from the dead all those times I'd prayed for her. The realization showed me the power we have as Christians that we often misunderstand or forget.

Next, I'd like to tell you about Tony. During a big prophetic conference at MorningStar Ministries, I met a family who promised to keep in touch with me afterward. The day after they left, I received an emergency phone call from them. They had just been in an accident, and their son Tony had been airlifted from the scene and had stopped breathing. I prayed for him with them, and it went something like this:

"Tony! Come back! It's not your time to die! We pull you back through the doors of death, and then slam them shut so that you can't go back through! We pray for divine intervention and miraculous healing for you, and command your body to respond—no ill effects for loss of oxygen to the brain and no ill physical effects. We pray in the power of the name and blood of Jesus Christ. Lord, we ask You that he will wake up like a child does after a fever, saying he's hungry."

Two hours later, the family called me again. Tony had survived. He woke up and said, "I'm hungry!"

The Limitless Possibilities of Prophecy

As you see, there are many ways to receive words for healing, deliverance, counseling, and even raising the dead. If we will listen, trust, and obey, God will direct us.

PRAYER

Dear Lord, we know You love Your people and desire for them to be healed, delivered, and made whole. Please use us to accomplish these things. We will be sure to give You all the glory. In Jesus's name, amen.

14

PROPHETIC DREAMS
AND THEIR INTERPRETATION

*For God may speak in one way, or in another, yet man does not
perceive it. In a dream, in a vision of the night, when deep sleep falls
upon men, while slumbering on their beds, then He opens the ears of
men, and seals their instruction. In order to turn man from his deed,
and conceal pride from man, He keeps back his soul from the Pit, and
his life from perishing by the sword.*
—Job 33:14–18

Pay Attention to Your Dreams

Increasing levels of revelation are coming forth, and much of it is being communicated through dreams. One of the reasons is because our dreams bypass our mind, will, and emotions. Many people lead such busy lives that they are unreachable by God, unable to hear from Him, during waking hours.

As we see, both the Old and New Testaments foretell such a season. Let's compare the corresponding prophecies now:

And it shall come to pass afterward that I will pour out My Spirit on all flesh; your sons and your daughters shall prophesy, your old men shall dream dreams, your young men shall see visions. (Joel 2:28)

And it shall come to pass in the last days, says God, that I will pour out of My Spirit on all flesh; your sons and your daughters shall prophesy, your young men shall see visions, your old men shall dream dreams.
(Acts 2:17)

God often uses our dreams to heal us of things we may not want to address when awake. Often, He will use them to release direction and purpose. Many inventions, medicines, cures for diseases, songs, business plans, works of art and literature, movie ideas, and more have been birthed as the result of dreams.[21] At times, while slumbering, we may even experience a visitation from the Lord that changes our entire life.

The content of our dreams is not always a message meant for the entire body of Christ. Most dreams are intended to help the dreamer deal with a wide range of personal issues. By paying attention to the message within the dream, one may receive the inner healing God intends for him or her.

As you seek God for answers and clarifications, be alert to the fact that He may release such information to you through a dream.

Many prophetic dreams from years past are about to be fulfilled. Timing is everything.

Some people are having "end-time dreams" foretelling what lies ahead for the church as we come to the end of an age.

We should always strive to hear God's voice, whether He speaks while we are awake or asleep.

While it is important to avoid overanalyzing one's dreams, we should also try not to second-guess ourselves all the time. Most dreams are not literal; they require interpretation. And for that, we should go directly to God rather than phoning a friend.

---

21. http://dreamtraining.blogspot.com/2010/12/inventions-that-came-in-dreams-largest.html?m=1 (accessed June 8, 2018).

Often, when people contact me for help in interpreting a dream, they already have a sense of the dream's meaning. They usually say something like, "Well, actually, I thought it meant such and such."

GOD OFTEN SPEAKS TO US IN THE SAME WAY
THAT WE SPEAK AND COMPREHEND THINGS.
IT'S HIS DESIRE FOR US TO UNDERSTAND HIM
SO THAT WE MIGHT OBEY HIM. IT ISN'T HIS
HEART TO CONFUSE US.

God often speaks to us in the same way that we speak and comprehend things. It's His desire for us to understand Him so that we might obey Him. It isn't His heart to confuse us.

Jesus—not me or anyone else—is the one mediator between God and Man. (See 1 Timothy 2:5.) He wants you to hear from Him for yourself.

God loves you and desires to have intimate communication with you. He may give you a dream that will prompt you to pray and to do research, because He knows what will work to draw you further into His Word and closer to Him.

Bad Dreams/Nightmares

God is not a terrorist. He's not into scaring or threatening His children. Thus, any bad dreams or nightmares are *not* from Him.

Consider the following Scriptures as additional proof of this truth:

He gives His beloved sleep.   (Psalm 127:2)

I will both lie down in peace, and sleep; for You alone, O LORD, *make me dwell in safety.*   (Psalm 4:8)

I lay down and slept; I awoke, for the LORD sustained me.

(Psalm 3:5)

If you are a prophetic dreamer, the enemy may attack you by inducing bad dreams in an effort to scare you away from dreaming. Never accept the lies of the enemy but pray over the area where you sleep, and proclaim the aforementioned Scriptures over yourself and your dream life.

We also must realize that not every dream we dream is from the Lord. Not every dream we dream has a deeper meaning that requires interpretation. We should never act upon a dream without first praying and seeking wise counsel from the Lord, as well as God-fearing people we trust. James 1:5 encourages us, *"If any of you lacks wisdom, let him ask of God, who gives to all liberally and without reproach, and it will be given to him."* The more we journal and ask God about our dreams, the more discernment we will obtain regarding their meaning.

There are myriad factors, many of them very simple, that can affect one's dream life—consumption of certain foods and beverages, exposure to medications and chemicals, stress, the viewing of movies or TV programs, and even the sounds and smells of the environment where one sleeps. As we take note of these types of details, our discernment and ability to interpret our dreams will improve.

When you travel and must spend the night away from home, be sure to pray a cleansing prayer over your hotel room or lodging. After you have ministered, pray to remove any hitchhiking spirits off yourself. Whenever a number of people come to your home for a house group meeting, ministry event, or other reason, pray over your home and your family members before retiring for the night. You can pray something like, "In Jesus's name, I command all hitchhiking spirits off me and my family/traveling companions/pets, and out of my home/hotel room."

The more diligent you are about journaling, praying over, and asking the Lord to clarify your dreams, the more dreams He will entrust to you. The faithfulness of God responds to our own faithfulness.

Be sure that any books you read on the subject of dream interpretation have been authored by Christians. Secular books on dream interpretation offer insights that are worldly and/or sexual in nature.

Dreams—those that are memorable as well as those that are forgotten—occur during the rapid eye movement (REM) sleep cycle.[22] If you are having trouble remembering your dreams, or if you would like to dream more often, ask God for help. He promises that if we ask, we will receive. (See Matthew 7:8.) Interestingly, it is said that a lack of vitamin B6 is often at the root of not being able to remember our dreams.[23]

Déjà Vu

Have you ever had the feeling of having already experienced something that you know you are really going through for the first time? This sense of familiarity with new events is called déjà vu. When this occurs, it may be that you are experiencing a situation that you previously dreamed about in detail.

In some cases, déjà vu gives us a heads-up so that we can take action to change the outcome of a situation we experienced in a dream. This has been my experience. My children and I once vacationed at a friend's cabin in Moravian Falls, North Carolina. I'd never been there before, nor had I been to the nearby town of Boone, where I decided we should go one day to have lunch and do some sightseeing.

When we arrived in Boone and exited the car, I had a flashback to a dream. I told my kids about the merchandise in several stores in the town, and then we visited those stores and saw the very items I had described, including a selection of imitation shrunken heads—not something I ever would have expected to see, had I not dreamed about it.

Another time, I found myself in a situation with a person when I suddenly realized I'd dreamed about it before. In the dream, I had had a big fight with this person. So, I left early in order to avoid having the bad part of my dream come to pass.

---

22. See Ed Jong, "Sleeping on it—how REM sleep boosts creative problem-solving," *Discover* magazine online, June 10, 2009. http://blogs.discovermagazine.com/notrocketscience/2009/06/10/sleeping-on-it-how-rem-sleep-boosts-creative-problem-solving/#.WZDj61GGPIU (accessed June 8, 2018).
23. Lindsay Dodgson, "This is the one vitamin you should take if you want to remember your dreams," *Business Insider*, April 30, 2018. https://amp.businessinsider.com/vitamin-b6-can-help-you-remember-your-dreams-2018-4 (accessed July 19, 2018).

We may also experience *lucid dreams*, in which we become aware that we are dreaming without waking up, and are able to take action to alter the outcome of the dream while still asleep.

Interpretation

Sleep restores the body, mind, and spirit. God wants to use our sleeping dreams to restore our ability to dream in life—to pursue the desires and accomplishments for which He put us on this earth. But dreaming is not helpful if we do not write down what we have seen and then seek its interpretation.

I learned from Prophet Bob Jones that the first moments when we awaken are the most crucial for recalling and recording our dreams, as well as for hearing from the Lord. It doesn't take long for the sights, sounds, and events of our day to crowd out the memory of our nighttime dreams. Consider making a practice of lying still with your eyes closed for a moment when you first wake up in the morning. During this time, try not to entertain any thoughts but patiently endeavor to recall, and then record, whatever the Lord may bring to mind.

It may be helpful to keep a digital recorder or a notepad and pen at your bedside to enable you to record your dreams as soon as possible. Make sure you list all identifying information, including the date and time, and include every detail you can recall about the dream—the setting, people, and events—as well as any thoughts you may have about the interpretation. Don't forget to log information about the weather, colors, symbols, and names. Try to recall any words or phrases that you heard or saw.

Once you've written a detailed account of your dream, review it and make a short outline of the most important aspects. Then, examine what you've recorded or written, and pray over it for further revelation. What meaning, if any, can you decipher from the symbols, numbers, colors, names, and so forth?

Children with the gift of prophecy often dream of flying, which is a sign of their revelatory gifting—soaring in spiritual realms.

If you dream of numbers on a clock, consider looking up a corresponding Scripture. For instance, the time of 3:33 might refer to Jeremiah 33:3.

Something in the dream may signify something else. I once had a dream that a big dog—specifically, a German shepherd—came to my home. This dog sat at my table and ate, then relaxed on my couch. Not too long after I had this dream, a pastor (or shepherd) from Germany visited our area and came to my home. I cooked dinner, and then we sat in my living room and conversed for hours.

A friend of mine dreamed about an unkind person whose arm she tore off. God spoke to her through this dream, telling her that He would help her disarm her enemies.

Some dreams are literal and need no interpretation, but most of them require some type of clarification.

The following are some highly recommended resources for help with dream interpretation.

+ *The Name Book*, by Dorothy Astoria

+ *Interpreting Types and Symbols*, by Kevin J. Conner

+ *Dreams and Visions*, by Jane Hamon

+ *Understanding the Dreams You Dream*, by Ira Milligan

+ *The Prophet's Dictionary*, by Paula Price

+ *Dictionary of Biblical Imagery*, edited by Leland Ryken, James C. Wilhoit, and Tremper Longman III

+ *The Divinity Code to Understanding Your Dreams and Visions*, by Adam F. Thompson and Adrian Beale

Recurring Dreams

If a dream repeats itself, it may be that God is trying to draw our attention to an area in which deliverance or healing is needed, or to a call He has for us.

There was a time when I consistently dreamed that I hadn't graduated from high school, even though I *had* already graduated—with honors! I even went back to school to earn a computer degree when my kids reached their teenage years, and I went on to get a doctorate in theology. A friend of mine interpreted this recurring dream, telling me, "You're the type of person that has such a thirst for knowledge and truth that you will never be done learning." Very accurate.

A recurring dream can also mean that a matter has been established by God and that He will act on it soon, as was the case in Genesis 41:32: *"And the dream was repeated to Pharaoh twice because the thing is established by God, and God will shortly bring it to pass."*

Parables and Types

Jesus often told parables as He taught. I believe the Lord sometimes chooses to give us dreams in the forms of parables, metaphors, copies, types, shadows, patterns, and mysteries we don't fully understand, in order to lead us on a greater path of discovery in His Word. As we search out the interpretation, He reveals Himself to us in a greater dimension. It says in Proverbs 25:2, *"It is the glory of God to conceal a matter, but the glory of kings is to search out a matter."*

If I grow frustrated while trying to discern an interpretation, I pray the Word of God out loud: "God, You said there is nothing hidden that will not be revealed, nor has anything been kept secret but that it should come to light. I have ears to hear, so let me hear." (See Mark 4:22–23.)

Most importantly, ask God for the interpretation. This advice may sound too simple, but in Genesis 40:8, Joseph rightly says that interpretation belongs to God.

I believe God uses balance in giving us dreams and prophetic words in order to protect us. He says in Ecclesiastes 5:7, *"For in the multitude of dreams and many words there is also vanity. But fear God."*

Many Types of Dreams

God knows what we need and when we need it. Whether our need is correction or encouragement, He can use our dreams to reveal it to us. Sometimes, we just need to communicate with Him, and He will meet with us, simply to fill us with His love. He will give us the wisdom, direction, and the courage we need to carry on in difficult times through these intimate encounters.

Not all bad dreams have negative interpretations. One time, a student at MorningStar had a dream that he came to my office at Derek Prince Ministries, and I was lying dead in a coffin behind my desk. He freaked out and went to talk to one of our leaders at MorningStar. The leader said, "She's not *physically* dying. She's dying to that part of her life. God has other things for her to do." Sure enough, that's when the Lord began opening the door for me to step into my own ministry.

GOD KNOWS WHAT WE NEED AND WHEN WE NEED IT. WHETHER OUR NEED IS CORRECTION OR ENCOURAGEMENT, HE CAN USE OUR DREAMS TO REVEAL IT TO US.

Some people are known for their prophetic dreams about the deaths of other people. One man came to me and told me his wife dreamed like that, and she'd recently had a dream of him dying, so he knew his time was up. God showed me that his wife had the opportunity to pray against her husband's death, so I told her that she ought to pray. She refused, as she was proud of her accuracy in prophesying death. Her husband *did* die soon thereafter. I believe the wife could have prevented that from happening at that time.

If someone comes to you with this type of verbal curse, pray against it, breaking its power. Declare that the person is simply moving into a new phase of life, like a butterfly breaking out of its chrysalis.

Whenever I have a dream about the death of someone, I take it as a warning of the enemy's plan and an assignment for intercession. I say, "Not on my watch, in Jesus's name!" Then I war in prayer against the vision. Never do I approach a person and declare his or her death to be imminent.

You do not have to accept verbal curses via prophetic words *or* dreams.

To bring balance to our discussion, let me say that God may choose to notify us when a loved one is about to pass away, in order to prepare us for the loss of that person. Trust God and yourself that you will know the difference.

False Dreams

There are such things as false dreams. The Bible says in Zechariah 10:2, "*For the idols speak delusion; the diviners envision lies, and tell **false dreams**; they comfort in vain. Therefore the people wend their way like sheep; they are in trouble because there is no shepherd.*"

Be aware of the enemy's plots to bring fear or division by inducing false dreams. False dreams are nothing to fear; just pray and ask the Lord to reveal the truth to you, and He will. Then, pray against the false dream, trusting God to protect you.

Dare to Dream

One of the dictionary definitions of *dreamer* is "one who has ideas or conceives projects regarded as impractical: visionary."

Imagination is the seedbed of creativity. The imaginations of such individuals as Walt Disney, Steve Jobs, and Bill Gates continue to touch countless lives. Many inventors had ideas and conceived of projects through dreams that others thought of as impractical or impossible.[24]

A *visionary* is defined as "one having unusual foresight and imagination."

The Bible says, "*Where there is no vision, the people perish*" (Proverbs 29:18 KJV).

If you've lost your vision or ability to dream, may God bring restoration to you. God made you to be a dreamer—that's why you're reading this book. I speak faith and a greater awakening of the anointing of dreams, visions, and hope inside you, by the power of the name and the blood of Jesus.

---

24. http://dreamtraining.blogspot.com/2010/12/inventions-that-came-in-dreams-largest. html?m=1 (accessed June 8, 2018).

PRAYER

Father, please touch each person who reads these words. Impart to us all renewed courage, faith, power, and anointing to have dreams, visions, interpretations, and victory in all we do for You and by Your power. In Jesus's name, amen.

15

PROPHESYING TO
THE SEVEN MOUNTAINS

You may or may not be familiar with a concept known as the Seven Mountains of Influence. According to www.the7mountains.com, there are seven pillars of society in which God is enabling His people to exert influence on the world: Family, Spirituality, Government, Celebration, Media, Education, and Economy.

In Luke 14:23, speaking through a parable, Jesus commands His disciples to *"go out into the highways and hedges, and compel them to come in, that my house may be filled."* It's time for us to go outside the church walls into the harvest field—the highways and hedges; the Seven Mountains of influence—and compel other people to come into the kingdom. Simply put, the Seven Mountains are the places where we live, work, eat, and play.

Let's explore this idea further by taking a closer look at each of the Seven Mountains.

The Mountain of Family

We are all called, at least to a certain degree, to the Family Mountain; each of us has a family, after all. For all the familiarity engendered by this relationship, we may find that our family members are the most difficult people to reach. Just as most of Jesus's friends and family did not acknowledge His authority or heed His teachings (see Matthew 13:57; Mark 6:4), our own family and friends may struggle the most to hear us. Our greatest ministry to them may be to simply love and pray for them without judging them.

We can speak to them prophetically without being religious about it. Because prophecy is for the purposes of edification, exhortation, and comfort, we can remind our loved ones of their skills, abilities, and good traits, and can encourage them to pursue their dreams.

WE MAY FIND THAT OUR FAMILY MEMBERS ARE THE MOST DIFFICULT PEOPLE TO REACH. JUST AS MOST OF JESUS'S FRIENDS AND FAMILY DID NOT ACKNOWLEDGE HIS AUTHORITY OR HEED HIS TEACHINGS, OUR OWN FAMILY AND FRIENDS MAY STRUGGLE THE MOST TO HEAR US.

Nobody wants the Bible crammed down his throat—not even a fellow Christian believer. We need to "be" Jesus to one another, not just preach Him.

Quite often, as our family members face challenging circumstances, they will turn to us for prayer, whether or not they are saved. When this occurs, we have an open door to do a bit of ministry. But we are more likely to catch their attention as we show interest in them as individuals rather than preaching at them. Loving relationships help develop others' trust in you, eventually opening doors for them to hear and accept the gospel message.

The Mountain of Spirituality

The church is a wonderful place for believers to come together and share their faith. Yet, all too often, this environment alienates those who are new to the Christian faith and/or those who are experiencing difficulties. Why? Because the church is often the place where the most judgmental groups of people are found.

In order to be effective in discipling those on the Mountain of Spirituality, we need to make the church a place of refuge where people can count on experiencing God's unconditional love. It should be a place where we help others grow in their faith and gain the strength to make it through their daily lives, as well as to discover their own God-given purpose and personal ministry.

If we are to keep the church alive, as a thriving organism, each person needs to be a working part of it. Then God will give us prophetic words to encourage those around us.

As we get to know those who labor among us, we will become more quickly aware when someone is on the verge of moving in a wrong direction. At such times, it is vital to handle our friends with care and pull them back into the fold, not condemn them and chase them away.

Sadly, many people come and go in our churches because no one speaks to them, let alone invites them to meet outside of church for fellowship or a meal. Every time someone new comes through the church doors, we have the opportunity to help keep that person in the love of God and to usher him or her to heaven with us. It's our job to let others know that we see and care about them.

Again, if we are to be effective in exerting influence on the mountain of Spirituality, we must do so in love, making it a place of refuge, not pain.

The Mountain of Government

The idea that the church should stay out of governmental affairs is false. If we read our Bibles, we see that God wants His people involved in government. He always sent His prophets to the leaders of nations to minister His will to them. He never told the prophets to stay out of politics. Governmental leaders should acknowledge having been placed in their positions of authority by God (see, for example, Daniel 2:21), and they should feel comfortable calling on His help to do their job.

The idea of the separation of church and state is not found in the Bible, nor does it come across in the Constitution of the United States of America. The phrase "separation between church and state" came from a letter written by Thomas Jefferson in 1802[25] to keep the government out of the

---

25. https://www.boundless.com/u-s-history/textbooks/boundless-u-s-history-textbook/founding-a-nation-1783-1789-9/ratification-and-the-bill-of-rights-80/separating-church-and-state-1381-9444/ (accessed June 8, 2018).

church's business, not vice versa. It was addressed to the Danbury Baptist Association in Connecticut, then published in a Massachusetts newspaper.

Jefferson wrote, "I contemplate with sovereign reverence that act of the whole American people which declared that their legislature should 'make no law respecting an establishment of religion, or prohibiting the free exercise thereof,' thus building a wall of separation between Church and State."[26]

Jefferson echoed the language of the founder of the First Baptist church in America, Roger Williams, who had written, in 1644, "[A] hedge or wall of separation between the garden of the church and the wilderness of the world."[27]

The letter was simply meant to uphold the church's right to exist and practice its beliefs without government interference or rule.

Throughout the Bible, we see God sending His prophets to anoint those coming into governmental office and to counsel those already there.

One year, during the time of a presidential election, I was in California on a ministry trip. I lived in the Carolinas, so I argued with God and myself about traveling home to cast my vote. I thought, *Why should I go all the way home to vote? The Word says God puts those in authority that need to be there.*

Soon the Lord began to help me understand that while He appointed certain people to positions of authority in Bible times, we are not to blame Him for the decisions we make in our elections. God judges the hearts of U.S. citizens every time we vote. If we vote to put someone in office who supports ungodly practices, such as abortion, we are at least partially responsible for every ungodly act along those lines taken during that person's term.

Even if none of the candidates running for a specific office seems all that great, we must vote against the most unlawful one.

As we pray for, vote in, and minister to those in government, our nation will be blessed.

---

26. https://www.boundless.com/u-s-history/textbooks/boundless-u-s-history-textbook/founding-a-nation-1783-1789-9/ratification-and-the-bill-of-rights-80/separating-church-and-state-1381-9444/ (accessed June 8, 2018).
27. Ibid.

The Mountain of Celebration (Including Arts, Entertainment, and Sports)

The Levitical Tabernacle of David is being restored, as God promised it would be, and the area of the arts is playing a big part in this restoration. I did a study in which I pulled up every Scripture relating to the words "Levite," "Levites," and "Levitical," and discovered that these terms do not merely refer to musicians and singers; other types of skilled artisans are included, such as bakers, jewelers, drapery makers, and the like. In this day, there are also many skilled artisans in the arenas of entertainment and sports.

Hollywood, representing the entertainment industry at large, has gotten a bad rap due in part to a religious spirit that demands that anyone there who gets saved must depart entirely from that realm. How crazy is that notion? If all the saved people leave, show business will only grow darker.

Many people involved in arts, entertainment, and sports are ripe for harvesting. We can reach them if we do not attempt to do it in a religious-spirited way. These people need to know that God loves them, that it is He who has given them their particular gifting, and that He is concerned with their personal lives. Too many of them suffer drug addition, bad relationships, successive divorces, and even suicide.

An underground move of God is occurring in Hollywood by which many people are coming to the Lord. Currently, there is a group of famous young "stars" who are privately renting space at various locations in order to meet and simply worship and seek the will of the Lord all night long. They want more of Jesus, and they are determined to get it.

People in the industries of arts, entertainment, sports, and so forth are hungry for the Lord, and God has promised a great move in their midst. Pray for those people whom the Lord lays on your heart.

For years, I prayed for the late singer/songwriter and "King of Pop" Michael Jackson. After he died, I found out that some people I know had ministered to and brought him to the Lord shortly before his death.

God is not going to ignore the Mountain of Celebration, and neither should we. It's a great harvest field for the Lord.

The Mountain of Media

There is a lot of talk these days about the media. Sadly, those in the industry who are unscrupulous have earned it a bad name. But you need to know, God would not leave them out of His kingdom.

I have met and ministered to many people involved in the news media who are hungry for the Lord. There *are* Christian believers among them.

I once received an e-mail from a lady in Atlanta whose son worked for CNN. This woman had forwarded her son an encouraging e-mail I had sent out, and her son sent it out to many of his associates. The message so touched him and his friends that they attended church with his mother that weekend and gave their lives to the Lord.

One time, I did a local meeting in Charlotte, North Carolina. The Lord gave me words for an attractive lady in the back of the room. After the meeting, she came to the front to meet me, and I learned that she was one of the lead TV newscasters in the Charlotte area. We developed a friendship, and she attended many of my meetings after that. She said the general public has no idea of what is really happening in the world, while those who report the news see hours upon hours of news footage that would cause great panic if the general society knew about it. As a result, she said, those who work for the news media desperately need encouragement, and she asked that we all pray diligently for them.

The Mountain of Education

There are many Christian educators in America, even in the secular school system, and they are as frustrated as the rest of us about the condition of our country. They teach because they are called to the profession, and they diligently pray for the children in their care. At the same time, they are disrespected, beat up, and spat upon; but that is their mission field. We need to pray for them. They are God's "secret agents" who lovingly protect the children of this nation—the next generation.

God has called Christian teachers to speak life and hope over their students. They have to do it in a way that is not obvious, but they accomplish it nonetheless.

Witches and demonic doctrines have infiltrated the educational systems of America. When I was employed by a Christian radio station owned by The Christian Broadcasting Network (CBN), we helped to expose some of the curriculum that had been infused with these doctrines. We need to pay attention to what our kids are being taught.

WE NEED TO PRAY FOR CHRISTIAN EDUCATORS. THEY ARE GOD'S "SECRET AGENTS" WHO LOVINGLY PROTECT THE CHILDREN OF THIS NATION— THE NEXT GENERATION.

Similarly, college campuses have been invaded by the belief systems of socialism and communism, in addition to the indoctrination of students with the skills of witchcraft.

If you are a Christian educator, know that God is with you and for you, and your job is of priceless value. You are helping to raise up the next generation that will lead our nation. Don't allow the enemy to discourage you. Persevere faithfully in your call, and your reward will be great.

May God remind the rest of us to pray for our educators and our school systems, as well as our students.

The Mountain of Economy (Including Business and Technology)

God has commissioned many people into marketplace ministry, placing them there to lead others into the kingdom, as well as to prosper. The Lord gives to them the knowledge, skills, and confidence to take godly risks for His purposes. They are the kingdom movers and shakers of our day.

God has business plans and witty inventions that He wants to prophetically release to His kingdom marketplace leaders. He is sending out His marketplace ministers to bring forth a great harvest. He will reveal business trends and future turns in the road, as well as give ideas and strategies to help change many lives. He is releasing to these leaders secrets that will influence the economies of many peoples and nations.

God has called many ministers out of the church to go into the marketplace. There they will bring in the big haul of souls that did not occur inside the church. These faithful shepherds will pastor, mentor, and train up other marketplace ministers. The marketplace will yield the greatest harvest of our day!

Many who have had apostolic anointings prophesied over them will fulfill those prophecies in the marketplace. They will parent the next generation to have the heart to work diligently and with integrity, to provide their generation with the ability to succeed as godly workplace mentors.

Remember Who Made the Mountains

Don't get pulled into a false "kingdom now" theology. We are not building our own kingdom or sphere of influence but God's. We must give Him the glory and take our mountain, or our personal sphere of influence, for Him rather than for ourselves. He is the only true King of any mountain. After all, He made each and every one of them. (See Amos 4:13.)

PRAYER

Dear Lord, please help us to understand and work with You as You lead us to take the mountains to which You send us. Give us Your wisdom, direction, anointing, and help. May we be found faithful. In Jesus's name, amen.

16

SUFFERING PERSECUTION FOR THE PROPHETIC GIFT

The enemy's hate-filled battle against God's prophets and the prophetic can start before one is born. Quite often, those who have a prophetic call upon their lives will experience warfare from the womb. The enemy will try to abort them in any way he can, beginning at life's start and continuing throughout their lives. If a mother doesn't bow to the idea of abortion, the enemy may attempt to cause the umbilical cord to become wrapped around the baby's neck, or he may try to make the labor and delivery process so difficult that it nearly kills both mother and baby.

My son CJ is highly prophetic. When he had gone a month and a half past his due date, I finally insisted that the doctors help me deliver him. I was later told that if I had gone just twenty-four hours longer without birthing him, we both would have died. When CJ was born, I nearly passed away from hemorrhaging. The enemy has since tried many times to take out my son through a variety of accidents, serious injuries, drugs, and other incidents. The enemy of our souls hates us.

When we are gifted in the Lord and have a call upon our lives, there are bound to be others who aren't happy about it. Jesus talked about this reality in the gospel of John, saying, *"Remember the word that I said to you, 'A servant is not greater than his master.' If they persecuted Me, they will also persecute you. If they kept My word, they will keep yours also"* (John 15:20).

Sadly, sometimes, those who oppose us are a part of our own family, circle of friends, or church family. *"A man's enemies will be those of his own household"* (Matthew 10:36).

Thankfully, God has promised us, *"No weapon formed against you shall prosper"* (Isaiah 54:17). Just as He did for David, God will cause the plans of our enemies to fail. (See Psalm 27:2.)

Those who walk in a very strong prophetic mantle are often ridiculed, misunderstood, maligned, and rejected. It can be disconcerting to others that we are able to discern and read them and their circumstances. Rejection often comes with the territory.

When we have a prophetic gift, we can get in trouble without saying a word. Other people may sense, in the spirit, our act of discerning them. Because of that (and their own guilty consciences), they may even accuse us of making comments that we never actually verbalized. Welcome to the club, my friend.

If Jesus, the perfect Son of God, was persecuted, why would we fault-prone prophetic folks think we would be exempt from persecution? We read in 1 Peter 4:12, *"Beloved, do not think it strange concerning the fiery trial which is to try you, as though some strange thing happened to you."*

The good news is that God remains with us through it all to complete the work that He started in us. (See Philippians 1:6.)

It isn't what happens to us that matters nearly as much as how we handle it. We must not allow another person's opinion or attitude to determine our destiny. We should never allow anyone but God to have that kind of power.

WE MUST NOT ALLOW ANOTHER PERSON'S OPINION OR ATTITUDE TO DETERMINE OUR DESTINY. WE SHOULD NEVER ALLOW ANYONE BUT GOD TO HAVE THAT KIND OF POWER.

I love what Christian author and teacher Francis Frangipane once said: "To inoculate me from the praise of man, He baptized me in the criticism of man until I died to the control of man."[28]

As long as we are concerned about what others think of us, we are prey to their power and control. But when we no longer care about obtaining others' approval, we are free from having their opinions overpower and control us. That's a good thing.

Let's bring balance. To go totally in one direction or the other is not good. We need to please our employers, spouses, church leaders, and others, at least to some degree; but we cannot live life to please everyone else to a higher degree than God.

False Accusation

Many times, even if we've done everything "right," someone will turn on us. That happened to one lady I knew. As a young worship leader in a small church, she was being used mightily of God. A powerful move of God began to take place through her and the worship team she led.

One night, the pastor's wife had a dream that my friend was a witch. It was a false dream from the enemy, intended to cause division for the purpose of shutting down the move of God. In truth, the opposite had occurred: Witches had attacked the worship leader. But the church pastors were untrained in the prophetic, and they publicly accused her of being a witch, then dismissed her from the worship team. She felt devastated, and so did the church. The church leadership's actions accomplished the purposes of the enemy. The move of God got shut down, the church became divided, and my friend withdrew from her calling for many years.

The enemy does not play fair. He is *"the accuser of our brethren"* (Revelation 12:10), and he often uses weak people to help him destroy the lives of others. We can't afford to focus on the pain others have inflicted on us. We must forgive, overcome, and move on. God will open bigger and better things to us as we do.

---

28. Francis Frangipane, *The Shelter of the Most High* (Lake Mary, FL: Charisma House, 2008), 155.

Whatever Doesn't Kill Us...

As a young single mother, I was part of a fairly new nondenominational church. The pastor and his wife were my best friends—or so I thought. I did whatever I could for them. I cleaned their house, babysat their kids, styled the wife's hair, and helped with setup and cleanup for various events at the church. The couple hardly needed to mention a need, and I would jump on it. I loved them like family and enjoyed serving them.

Soon they appointed me to a position of authority over the home group leaders. I would hold meetings in my home during which I would teach those leaders the lesson that the pastors wanted them to teach their groups. God really showed up. We experienced miracles, healings, and deliverance. The power and presence of God were manifest. When the leaders began to testify about what had been going on, the pastors grew jealous. They shut down the meetings, removed me from my position, and falsely accused me of trying to take over the church.

It didn't stop there. The pastors told the men in the church to keep their wives away from me because I had a Jezebel spirit. Then they called in my kids, who attended the church's Christian school, and told them I was mentally ill, saying they planned to have me committed. They also told my kids not to obey me but to help them put me away so that the pastors could adopt them.

Needless to say, after my kids spilled the beans to me regarding the whole scheme, our family left that church. Terrified, I went to a large denominational church and sought help from the counseling team there. I submitted to them and told them everything. I asked them to find out if anything was wrong with me, adding that if they did, I wanted deliverance. The pastor and his team just laughed and told me I was just fine; the pastors of my former church were the crazy ones. My new pastor told me he'd been through a similar experience, then said, "Welcome to the club." He and the rest of the church leadership backed and protected me, and ended up inviting me on staff.

I've just shared only a few examples of persecution I have experienced in my walk with the Lord. If I told you about every instance of persecution, you might wonder why I stayed in the church. I did so because God put it in my heart to serve *Him* and not to allow myself to be taken out of commission by the enemy. It's important to do routine self-checks and to have people who will hold us accountable. I have a home church I attend when I'm not on the road, and I have people who hold me accountable. I didn't let what happened cause me to become a rogue who despises church, for how can we help the church if we despise her?

There's an old saying, "Whatever doesn't kill you makes you stronger." But that's true only if we adopt the proper attitude. We must not allow the lies and opinions of the enemy, other people, or even ourselves to destroy us.

Experience should be our teacher, not our trainer. Let's not allow the bad things people have done to become a pattern for us to follow.

Even if we suffer persecution, the goal is to keep our heart right so that our message will be pure.

Refused Insight

I moved cross-country to attend, serve, and be part of a wonderful ministry. My aim was to soak up the anointing there while serving and being a blessing in some way. The ministry was in the middle of a huge transition, and on one Sunday morning, they introduced a new head pastor.

During this introduction, the ministry leaders stood up front and put their arms around the man. I suddenly had a flash vision of the new pastor stabbing the ministry's main leader in the back. The image was so vivid that I gasped. I quickly wrote down what I had seen. I felt that the Lord was telling me to give the word to the ministry leader I had seen being stabbed, but to be mindful of the timing and to deliver the message privately.

Within the next few days, the opportunity presented itself. I gave the word verbally in person, as well as in written form. The leader laughed it off, saying that the whole leadership team had prayed about it and knew they had hired the right man for the job. The change had been solidified. The ministry leader thanked me for caring, then said he needed to get back to work.

Over the next several years, that church suffered badly. The new pastor tore things up and came against the ministry leader, trying to destroy him.

After being there a year, I left but continued to pray from a distance. In time, God removed the man with the spiritual knife in his hand, and straightened up the mess.

Our words won't always be received, heeded, *or* remembered. Someone may say, "I wish I would have listened to you," but that's unlikely. I've developed an attitude that says, "It's God's deal, not mine." Once I've done my part and have given the word, I'm done. I just pray privately and ask God to help him or her to clean things up when the roof falls in.

OUR WORDS WON'T ALWAYS BE RECEIVED, HEEDED, *OR* REMEMBERED.... ONCE I'VE DONE MY PART AND HAVE GIVEN THE WORD, I'M DONE. I JUST PRAY PRIVATELY AND ASK GOD TO HELP HIM OR HER TO CLEAN THINGS UP WHEN THE ROOF FALLS IN.

Another time, I gave a friend a word about being in business with a particular man. He applied my word to a different person. Nothing I could say would change his mind. A catastrophe occurred, and he blamed me for giving him a wrong word. I calmly explained that he had misunderstood my word and had chosen to apply it the way he wanted.

Another friend of mine was married to a successful Christian businessman. For five years, I warned her husband about his business partner, whose wife handled the books without any supervision from my friend's husband. When he finally took my advice and checked out the company's finances, he discovered that his partner had been misusing their money for years.

There are some friends of mine I first met when someone asked me to minister over them, after which point they were continually asking me for a word—even though the familiarity between us, due to our friend-ship, meant that they disregarded anything I told them. They loved me but would brush off whatever I said. In fact, it often seemed they would automatically do the exact opposite of any advice I offered. Over and over, they ended up in trouble. I finally told them that I would pray for them but would not give them any more prophetic words because I felt we were too close for that. In truth, I grew tired of feeling responsible for their suffering because of their propensity to do the opposite of whatever I spoke.

Just as Jesus was not received in His own hometown (see Matthew 13:57; Mark 6:4), the tyranny of the familiar will sometimes cause our voice to go unheard by those closest to us. We have to get over that, and pray for them. We are not to be anyone's personal Holy Spirit. We must maintain an attitude of integrity and a heart of joy in spite of everything.

Well Done

All of us desire to hear our heavenly Father say to us, *"Well done, good and faithful servant"* (Matthew 25:21, 23).

We sometimes suffer persecution that we don't deserve. It will happen to us all at some point, but we have to keep moving forward and not allow it to destroy us.

When we attend a church, the leadership deserves our respect and honor. We are not the head; they are. Anything with more than one head is a monster. Just because we may receive a few prophetic words, it does not promote us to being the pastor's boss. If we work for Walmart as a cashier, the manager is in charge, even if we should become a department head.

It never ceases to amaze me how some people, especially those with a prophetic bent, believe that they occupy a position of authority over their church pastor because of a few prophetic words they receive. Does the mail carrier become the head of our household because he delivers our mail? Of course not.

Manners and common sense are vital as we try to work together. We should honor those in authority in the church the same way we would honor our boss in a secular job. Just because someone comes over for din-ner, we would not let that person usurp our authority as the head of our household. Likewise, when we dine on the Word at our local church, that does not promote us above the leaders there.

A Short Rant

Some prophetic ministries teach and activate people in prophetic ministry who immediately refer to each person they train as a "prophet." This practice is a recipe for disaster. To give everyone the title of prophet is wrong, out of order, and downright crazy.

I've seen some of those people go home to their churches all puffed up with pride at their new title and wreak havoc. If you teach about the prophetic, please don't do that to them or to those pastors and churches. Titles are greatly overrated and misunderstood. We who are in the church, no matter what our position may be, should always seek to serve one another, not enslave them.

There's enough persecution of prophetic people without us contributing to it. Let's be full of the love and kindness of the Lord and His fruits as we minister our gifts. Let's seek to give of ourselves without recognition or recompense. God Himself will be our reward.

PRAYER

Dear Lord, please help those of us who have gone through persecution to be healed and to get over it. Help us to become shining examples of Your love as we use your gifts. Heal us all from the persecutions we have received, and please help us to avoid inflicting persecution on others. In Jesus's name, amen.

17

GUARDING AGAINST DECEPTION

There is a difference between the true prophetic—that which is from the Lord—and the false prophetic. God is the Creator who makes the real. The enemy has no power to create; all he can do is tell lies. Jesus described him this way in John 8:44:

> He was a murderer from the beginning, and does not stand in the truth, because there is no truth in him. When he speaks a lie, he speaks from his own resources, for he is a liar and the father of it.

Satan, our enemy, offers counterfeit gifts that oppose the Lord's purposes. The differences between the true prophetic and the "prophetic" of the enemy lie in their *source* and *motive*.

The true prophetic, which proceeds from the heart of God, seeks to edify and encourage (see 1 Corinthians 14:3), bringing the fulfillment of God's heart and plans for us, and freedom from the enemy's plans. Whoever has been set free by the Son is free indeed. (See John 8:36.) The enemy's counterfeit includes all areas of divination, which puts a divining hook in its victims to control and manipulate them. Divination involves communicating and playing games with demonic entities, including fortune-telling, tarot cards, horoscopes, clairvoyance, Ouija boards, necromancy, and so forth.

God does not want us to be ignorant of what He has to offer us, and neither does He want us to be ignorant of the enemy's devices. (See 1 Corinthians 2:11; 12:1.) Our God is not dead, nor is He deaf or mute.

He longs to communicate and impart His gifts and knowledge to His children. As Jesus said, *"If you then, being evil, know how to give good gifts to your children, how much more will your Father who is in heaven give good things to those who ask Him!"* (Matthew 7:11).

God would never identify as wrong or sinful something good just so He can keep it from us. Rather, He wants to protect us from evil. Therefore, we should follow the injunction of Hebrews 12:25: *"Do not refuse Him who speaks."*

Some people *willfully* and *purposely* ignore the intelligence of God that is presented to them either through His written Word or through His prophetic word. They refuse the directives He offers and go their own way, thereby suffering separation from Him and His blessings.

The consequences of dabbling in the enemy's games are great, as we realize upon reading Deuteronomy 18:9–12:

> *When you come into the land which the* LORD *your God is giving you, you shall not learn to follow the abominations of those nations. There shall not be found among you anyone who makes his son or his daughter pass through the fire* [an ancient occult practice], *or one who practices witchcraft, or a soothsayer, or one who interprets omens, or a sorcerer, or one who conjures spells, or a medium, or a spiritist, or one who calls up the dead. For all who do these things are an abomination to the* LORD*....*

Nobody desires to be an abomination to the Lord—someone whom God finds detestable.

God encourages us to use the gifts He gives to us. However, because He loves us, He desires for us to use discernment and to refrain from going to the dark side, which may result in bringing a curse upon our lives, not to mention eternity in hell.

A Word of Hope

Some people get caught up in the practice of deception because they want to be thought of as important by seeming able to do things that others cannot. Such individuals are not necessarily evil but may just desire attention. This is one way in which the enemy may establish a foothold. But sin is sin.

Other people knowingly operate by deception with ungodly motives. I knew of a man doing just that, with the underlying purpose of extracting financial support from his victims. A liar and a con artist, he operated in familiar spirits in order to entice his prey.

Don't beat yourself up if you have become a victim of deception, but please pray for God-given discernment, that you may not fall prey to the spirit of deception again.

If we reject the truth, we perish for lack of knowledge. (See Hosea 4:6.) Thankfully, it is possible to repent and to receive forgiveness from God. After that, we can bring others to the truth. There is redemption for offenders of deception, just as there is for its victims, if they will merely seek it. God does not look to spoil our fun or to kill us. His desire is to cleanse us from unrighteousness so we can spend eternity with Him. *"If we confess our sins, [God] is faithful and just to forgive us our sins and to cleanse us from all unrighteousness"* (1 John 1:9).

The Holy Spirit is called the Spirit of truth. (See, for example, John 15:26.) The more we love truth, the more the Spirit of truth will love to reveal truth both to us and through us.

The Deception of Communicating with the Dead

The dictionary defines *necromancy* as "conjuration of the spirits of the dead for purposes of magically revealing the future or influencing the course of events; magic, sorcery." Anyone who claims to communicate with the dead is called a *medium*.

Jesus could communicate with the deceased because He is God. But He says that there is a gulf between the living and the dead that cannot be crossed in either direction. (See Luke 16:26.)

Second Corinthians 5:8 tells us that *"to be absent from the body and to be present with the Lord."* Simply put, if a believer dies, they are immediately with Jesus in heaven.

Hebrews 9:27 says, "*It is appointed for men to die once, but after this the judgment.*"

Therefore, whether one has gone on to heaven or hell, he or she is no longer available for contact by the living.

Additionally, Ecclesiastes 9:5–6 says, "*The living know that they will die; but the dead know nothing…nevermore will they have a share in anything done under the sun.*" There you have it, again: There is no earthly contact with someone after he or she has died.

THERE IS NO EARTHLY CONTACT WITH SOMEONE AFTER HE OR SHE HAS DIED.

So, what is really happening when certain individuals claim to be able to mediate between you and the spirits of your deceased loved ones? Such people are in communication with familiar *demonic* spirits who appear as angels of light (see 2 Corinthians 11:14) and attempt to control and manipulate with their information.

The following Scriptures specifically warn against the practice of necromancy:

You shall not…practice divination or soothsaying.   (Leviticus 19:26)

Give no regard to mediums and familiar spirits; do not seek after them, to be defiled by them: I am the LORD your God.   (Leviticus 19:31)

The person who turns to mediums and familiar spirits, to prostitute himself with them, I will set My face against that person and cut him off from his people.   (Leviticus 20:6)

That's strong language. When practicing necromancy, one prostitutes himself with familiar (demonic) spirits, or uses his talents in a base manner rather than in a way that is appropriate or respectable.

God is the giver of all good gifts (see James 1:17), but we have the free will to decide whether to utilize those gifts for His glory or to prostitute them for use by the enemy. We shall all one day stand before God to give an answer for our choice. (See 2 Corinthians 5:10.)

What About Ouija Boards?

Although I grew up attending church, our household was characterized by the type of mixture I'm talking about. My mother often went to fortune-tellers or psychics and kept such items as an eight ball and an Ouija board in our home. As you may know, Ouija boards operate by supposed contact with demonic spiritual forces—not something a Christian family should be using.

It always frightened me when someone would use the Ouija board, even though the spirits would usually refuse stubbornly to answer anyone's questions. I was the exception. Whenever I got involved—reluctantly—the planchette would fly all over the board. I'm convinced it did this because I had a prophetic gifting that the spirits wanted to own for themselves. Or maybe they wanted to own me.

Either way, the board gave me the creeps, and I finally refused to play with it. Soon after that, the Ouija board got stashed away in its box inside the closet of the room I shared with my sister. The demonic spirits apparently got mad at being ignored, for we would occasionally hear noises coming from the closet, as if the board were jumping up and down inside the box in an effort to get our attention. It was freaky.

After a while, I started experiencing serious demonic visitations at night, the fear of which kept me from sleeping. When my mother told our pastor about what was happening, he asked if we happened to have an Ouija board in the house. My mother said yes and explained to him how the board refused to operate unless I participated. The pastor decided the Ouija board was the source of the problem, and he offered to take care of the situation.

One day while I was at school, the pastor came to our house and, with the help of my mother and sister, burned the Ouija board in the backyard. According to my mother and sister, the board screamed and thrashed in the burn barrel, and they had to continually douse it with charcoal lighter fluid in order to incinerate it completely. The pastor then prayed over our home and anointed it, evicting any evil spirits.

At the same time the board was burning, I got sick with a fever at school, presumably as retaliation for our having burned the board. Once I returned home, I could sense the change in the atmosphere of my room. From that night on, I experienced undisturbed sleep.

Years later, after learning much more about the occult, I went through deliverance for any involvement with the demonic realm—an experience that has helped me to set others free from the same bondage. We don't need Ouija boards to "prophesy" to us. We have personal communication with the Creator of the universe.

When we repent, or turn from, divination in all its forms, we find forgiveness and hope in the name, blood, and life of Jesus Christ. The process may require you to endure a fierce battle, but your freedom is worth it. If those spirits try to return, command them, "Be gone, in Jesus's name!"

If you or a loved one has battled in the area of necromancy, divination, or demonic visitations, I encourage you to read one or all of the following books by Derek Prince: *Blessing or Curse, You Can Choose*; *Deliverance and Demonology*; *Healing Through Deliverance*; *They Shall Expel Demons*; *Bought with Blood*; and *Pulling Down Strongholds*.

What About People Who Claim to Communicate with the Apostles or with Deceased Famous Ministers?

The Bible talks about "third heaven" visits, in which people literally visit heaven. To my knowledge, this is the only scriptural way for such a thing to occur. I have no doubt that third-heaven visits can happen, especially in our dreams.

I once dreamed of meeting with three women on a street corner. As I looked at them, I recognized them as three deceased female evangelists: Kathryn Kuhlman, Aimee Semple McPherson, and Maria

Woodworth-Etter. Kathryn Kuhlman led the conversation. Each woman had a ticket, and Aimee and Maria handed their tickets to Kathryn. She explained that they had talked it over, and each one had individually decided to give her ticket to me. I argued that I wasn't important enough. Kathryn said, "Stop talking foolishness and take them. We don't have time for this. We know what we're supposed to do."

I have yet to understand the gravity of that experience, but it was as real as if I was talking to you.

What About Those Who Lie on the Graves of Deceased Famous Ministers to Receive Impartation?

I don't know of any Scripture to back up or condone this practice—one that I personally find very creepy. The deceased person isn't in the grave; it's just his or her bones. I suggest avoiding this practice, lest it open the door to a spirit of death. We have access to the Holy Spirit to get direct impartation from Him. What could be better?

What About the Witch of Endor?

Invariably, when teaching on the danger of dark arts, someone brings up the account of Saul using a medium to speak to the spirit of the deceased prophet Samuel. (See 1 Samuel 28:3–25.) I will admit that this subject is one about which I'm not entirely clear. It is true that in 1 Samuel 28:7, Saul specifically asked for a medium, because God would no longer speak to him. It had already been established that no one was to consult witches or mediums, or speak to familiar demonic spirits. (See Leviticus 19:31; 20:27.) Therefore, we might surmise that what had actually been conjured up was a familiar spirit coming forth as an angel of light in the form of the prophet Samuel. However, from the way it is written, it seems that Saul actually spoke to Samuel.

My "answer" to this question is to say, let's not split hairs. The Bible instructs us not to attempt to play with demons or dead people. And why would we want to, when we have personal and complete access to the King of Kings and Lord of Lords?

The Deception of "Wandering Souls"

I was talking with someone who believes that people sometimes get stuck between life and death if their manner of dying was particularly dramatic, quick, or confusing. This person further believes we need to help such individuals "get things right" so they can go on into eternity. According to the Word of God, this belief is faulty. No death ever catches God by surprise, and the Bible tells us that to be absent from the body is to be present with the Lord. (See 2 Corinthians 5:8.)

One time, when I was presenting an argument against "wandering souls" at a church, a woman became so angry that she followed me from the room where I had been teaching and confronted me in the ladies' restroom. She told me that she knew her deceased mother had been talking to her, and she went on to recount how she'd once fallen asleep in a chair in her living room and had experienced a powerful visit in which her deceased mother ran in and shook her arm to wake and warn her that the turkey she had cooking in the oven was about to burn.

I tried to reason with this woman, telling her that I could not imagine God sending her mother from a peaceful place beside Him in heaven just to prevent her daughter's turkey from burning. I suggested that perhaps it had been an angel of the Lord, or the Holy Spirit, speaking to her. Even though it would be a stretch, I thought God might do something like that to protect her from a house fire that could have resulted from a burning turkey. But the woman refused to be persuaded.

Deception is defined as "the act of causing someone to accept as true or valid what is false or invalid." The spirit of deception is a lying spirit sent to the mind to convince it of the validity of a lie. But, as we have seen, the Bible is clear that earthly problems won't bother us in heaven.

A spirit of deception may attempt to convince us that someone can contact the dead at will. Whether the person is doing it for money or attention is irrelevant. It is deception. It is a lie. It is sin, and therefore not pleasing to God.

Jesus Himself has warned us, *"False Christs and false prophets will rise and show great signs and wonders to deceive, if possible, even the elect"* (Matthew 24:24).

The Deception of Sorcery

Galatians 5:20 names sorcery, or divination, as a work of the flesh. Verse 21 reinforces just how serious the consequences of practicing it are: *"I tell you beforehand, just as I also told you in time past, that **those who practice such things will not inherit the kingdom of God**"* (Galatians 5:21).

Once someone is convinced to take part in sorcery, it opens the door to other types of divination and witchcraft, the practice of which can wreak havoc in the home and bring in curses in the forms of frightening nightmares, demonic visitations, and so forth.

Many Christians are dabbling in divination, thereby bringing into the church a harmful degree of mixture that needs to be addressed.

UFOs, Nephilim, and Clones

Some people are beginning to get sensational with discussions about the Nephilim, cloning people, hybrid humanoids, extraterrestrial alien beings, UFO sightings, and the like. Let's focus on the Word and not get pulled away by the distractions of such nonsense.

Deceptions I Have Witnessed

Jesus warned that deception would come—deception so effective that it would threaten to manipulate the elect. (See Matthew 24:24.) No one is automatically immune to the devil's deception.

A Dishonest Televangelist

In my late twenties, the church I attended helped host a speaking engagement by a famous televangelist, for which it rented a 5,000-seat theater. Many of the church members volunteered to help, myself included.

When I arrived at the meeting, I found the evangelist's staff to be quite helpful. They grabbed wheelchairs and offered rides to the front row of the auditorium. They winked and said, "Being in one of these will give you a better view."

I unloaded products and did some other tasks I was assigned, then sat in the volunteers' area. There I met a lady who was in pain due to an automobile accident. I let the staff know she needed healing, and they assured me she would be prayed for.

The auditorium filled with excitement. The people were prompted to shout, "Jesus! Jesus! Jesus! Jesus!" and other cheers. There were competitions to see which section could shout the loudest. They were told their enthusiasm would encourage the evangelist to press into the anointing; conversely, they were warned that if they did not participate, it might prevent any miracles from happening. The service began, and the crowd did as directed.

For a while, the evangelist told stories of past miracles. Then a few people were brought onto the stage and were prayed for. The evangelist seemed to know everything about them.

The staff then fetched the lady I'd met who'd had the car accident.

"Watch and listen." Although I heard the words in my spirit rather than with my ears, the Lord spoke to me in a serious tone. "Watch and listen!" He said. "I'm going to teach you something tonight to carry with you for the rest of your life."

The evangelist asked the lady, "I've never spoken to you before, right?"

She responded, "No, but I spoke to your staff."

He asked her to simply answer either yes or no, and then he asked her again if she had ever had a conversation with him.

She said, "No."

He then began speaking of things she'd told his staff members, while acting like it was fresh revelation from God.

The lady began to cry and shake. She seemed nervous about the way he was handling things.

The evangelist took advantage of her physical reaction and said, "There it is! His anointing is on you right now!"

He asked those in the audience to stretch their hands toward her and agree for her healing. He then recited a healing Scripture, reminding everyone how God said that if two or more agree, He will do what is asked. (See Matthew 18:19.). He also spoke of the blood and name of Jesus.

He then told the lady to touch her toes and do things she couldn't do before, and she did. The audience applauded and jumped to their feet.

When the evangelist sent the woman to her seat, he walked over to the section of wheelchairs down in front and commanded those sitting in them to get up and walk. The crowd went wild. But I remembered that those people hadn't needed wheelchairs in the first place.

The Lord drew my attention back to the lady who had just gotten healed. He said, "See her face? She is grieved about how things occurred. What just happened here is that I honored My Word, My Son's blood and name, and the prayers and faith of My people. My Word does not go forth and return void. When five thousand people agree on My Word and in My Son's name,[29] people *will* get healed, but *not* because of the vessel.

"I'll deal with him in time," the Lord went on. "What occurred tonight is why My Word says that there will be those who may prophesy, heal, and cast out demons in My name, yet I'll tell them to depart from Me because I never knew them." (See Matthew 7:21–23.)

"Go tell her I love her, explain this, and tell her not to reject her healing because of him. I'm the One who gave it to her." (See Matthew 18:20; 7:21–23.)

The lady ran out of the auditorium, so I went after her as God had directed me. She wept and said, "I don't deserve to be healed! I helped him lie!"

The evangelist was later exposed for having received information via an earpiece while ministering, and he spent time in prison for other things.

A Strategic "Prophet"

One prophet who came to town had his assistant collect informational notes about certain people. He also obtained a copy of the conference registrants' names to "pray over." When the prophet stood in the pulpit, he spoke as if he had received people's names and information from the Lord. We can know some things in the natural and still give a rightful prophetic word. But it's important to operate with integrity and to say, for example,

---

29. Matthew 18:20.

"I know such and such in the natural, but, by the Spirit, I am receiving _____ about it."

One young man calls people out and tells them their dead loved ones are praying for them. As it turns out, one of his relatives made a career out of training mediums. This young man speaks with familiar (demonic) spirits, not actual deceased loved ones.

WE DON'T NEED TO CONFER WITH DEMONS. WE HAVE ACCESS TO COMMUNICATE WITH THE KING OF KINGS AND LORD OF LORDS.

Familiar spirits are just that—they are *familiar* with our lives because they have hung out around us and our relatives for generations. We don't need to confer with demons. We have access to communicate with the King of Kings and Lord of Lords.

The Gems

One man had a collection of bright neon-colored "gems," all the same size and cut, that he claimed angels had thrown to him. In actuality, God had given him a recipe similar to that for cubic zirconia to manufacture what looked like gems, for a business venture. This man misused the product to try to make a name for himself in church circles.

Quite a few prophetic ministries began claiming God delivered gems to certain people in their services. Some even had these gems examined, and they were real. I still don't feel right about it.

One day I received an e-mail from an eBay seller saying, "Many of your friends are buying gem pieces from me to use in their meetings, so I thought I'd see if you'd like to order them."

God can do *real* miracles. We don't need to fake anything. God could surely help us find a valuable diamond to pay our bills, if need be, just as Jesus found a fish with a coin in its mouth to pay His taxes. (See Matthew 17:24–27.) I just can't justify the idea of our loving God preferring to put on sideshows of randomly throwing gems to wow people in a meeting instead of healing someone dying a painful death of cancer.

Gold Dust

I've seen incidents in which a fleck or two of gold dust appeared on someone supernaturally. However, there was a pastor I watched become totally encrusted with gold as he ministered. I felt queasy about the sight, so cried out to the Spirit of truth to show me the truth.

Soon afterward, I received a phone call from a woman who told me her husband had been spraying that minister before each service with a clear, water-like mist used by magicians. As the substance dried under the hot lights used onstage during the meetings, it would manifest as a thick crust of gold-colored dust. This woman said she'd been having dreams similar to those of the wife of Pontius Pilate regarding the crucifixion of Jesus. (See Matthew 27:19.) In short, she knew the practice was displeasing to the Lord. I advised her and her husband to get out of the business they were doing, repent, and start attending a God-following church.

In another situation, a reputable pastor exposed a traveling lady minister who would run her fingers through her hair while ministering, releasing gold dust from packets hidden on her scalp so that it ran down her face. He advised the churches in his fellowship of ministries to have nothing to do with her.

Faked Holy Laughter

I believe that holy laughter is a legitimate spiritual experience. God delivered me of a spirit of suicide in the privacy of my own home by holy laughter. My experience was real, and the fruit of it saved my life.

Years later, there was a massive movement of laughter in the church that seemed to bear good fruit for a while. Many people were delivered of various strongholds, including depression, suicide, and a religious spirit.

But some people seemed addicted to producing this laughter long after its time had passed. The Bible says there is a time and a season for everything. (See Ecclesiastes 3:1.) This practice became so overdone that it became almost embarrassing to invite visitors to church, lest the widespread hilarity scare them away.

Many of those who consistently went after holy laughter invoked as justification the Bible verse in which Peter defends the behavior of those who have been baptized in the Holy Spirit, saying, *"These are not drunk, as you suppose"* (Acts 2:15). Such individuals are forgetting that Acts 2:15 refers to the practice of speaking in tongues. We do not have to twist the Scriptures, which 2 Peter 3:16 warns against, to justify what we are doing if it is genuine.

It always made me uncomfortable when uncontrollable laughter drowned out the voice of someone speaking to the congregation. I was raised to have manners and show respect to others, and such riotous displays seemed, to me, more like the evidence of a mocking spirit.

One night at my home church, only a few of us did not become "drunk with laughter." I didn't feel like laughing, and I wasn't about to fake it. I simply sat in the back and wrote in my journal. Suddenly, I felt two hands grab my shoulders and heard a female voice shout, "Laugh!"

I was so startled, I jumped and automatically pushed the hands away. "Don't do that!" I yelled. "You scared me!"

For about six weeks after that, I exhibited symptoms of a heart issue, to the extent that I saw a cardiologist and started wearing a heart monitor. One Saturday, I hosted a meeting of women from my church, including the woman who had startled me. The other women prayed for me regarding my condition. Later on, in the privacy of my kitchen, the woman who had startled me approached me and admitted that she'd felt angry and rejected because of the way I'd reacted at church. It turns out that she had been praying curses over me that I would have a heart attack. She apologized, and I forgave her.

On another occasion, I was traveling to a ministry event with an intercessor who was in to holy laughter. I had asked her if she would be able to control herself if she came along, and she'd promised me she could. However, as I prayed for a woman, the intercessor began to laugh uncontrollably. The woman thought the intercessor was laughing *at* her. I halted the time of ministry in order to apologize for the behavior of the intercessor, whom I then sent to sit in the car until I finished.

Afterward, I reminded the intercessor of her promise and asked her why she had laughed anyway. She replied that she didn't know; she "couldn't control it." I dismissed her response, reminding her this time that self-control is one of the fruits of the Holy Spirit. (See Galatians 5:22–23.) I then suggested that if she truly could not control her urge to laugh, it was due to either mental illness or a demon. She finally admitted to having had a problem with inappropriate laughter all her life, and said the laughing movement helped her hide it.

Holy laughter should not be confused with paradoxical laughter, which often indicates a mental condition.

WE MUST EXERCISE DISCERNMENT TO SEPARATE THE TRUE FROM THE FALSE. CHURCH LEADERS MUST HAVE THE COURAGE TO SPEAK UP AND PUT THINGS TO A STOP WHEN THE ENEMY TRIES TO MANIFEST A LIE.

There *is* genuine holy laughter that does not proceed from mental instability and does not need to be faked. We must exercise discernment to separate the true from the false. Church leaders must have the courage to speak up and put things to a stop when the enemy tries to manifest a lie.

Gold Teeth

I personally don't desire gold teeth, but some people do. At one conference I attended, there was talk of people's dental fillings' being replaced by gold. The report was supposedly verified.

A few months later, the truth came out. The person with the "verified" gold teeth did, in fact, have them—they had been put there by a dentist months before the conference.

Some people really have had gold fillings miraculously appear in their teeth. I believe that God can do dental work if He wants to spare someone from pain, infection, expense, and even death. But, again, we don't have to fake it if it's genuine.

The Bottom Line

It takes all kinds of people to minister to all kinds, but our God is Creator of the real. He doesn't need to fake anything.

The disciples didn't "follow signs"; signs followed them. Jesus said:

And these signs will follow those who believe: In My name they will cast out demons; they will speak with new tongues; they will take up serpents; and if they drink anything deadly, it will by no means hurt them; they will lay hands on the sick, and they will recover.

(Mark 16:17–18)

Those are the types of signs we should seek.

Even if something is happening "supernaturally," this does *not* make it "of God." That's why people become deceived. They think because they can't explain it, it must be of God. Jesus made it clear that not all signs and wonders are *of Him*. That's why He warned against *lying* signs, wonders, and some fakes. (See Matthew 7:22.) And we read in 2 Thessalonians the following sobering words:

The coming of the lawless one is according to the working of Satan, with all power, signs, and lying wonders, and with all unrighteous deception among those who perish, because they did not receive the love of the truth, that they might be saved. And for this reason God will send them strong delusion, that they should believe the lie, that they all may be condemned who did not believe the truth but had pleasure in unrighteousness. But we are bound to give thanks to God always for you, brethren beloved by the Lord, because God from the beginning chose you for salvation through sanctification by the Spirit and belief in the truth....   (2 Thessalonians 2:9–13)

Even so, no matter what, God honors His Word, His Son's shed blood and name, and the prayers and faith of His people. His Word does not go forth and return void. (See Isaiah 55:11.) God-ordained miracles *will* happen in spite of the vessels through whom they operate. But that doesn't make it okay for ministers and prophets to practice deception. Do not allow anyone to misuse the Scriptures to control or manipulate you. You would be bowing to spiritual abuse if you heed any warnings not to discern or speak up about such wrongdoings. It is up to us to discern and use the plumb line of God's Word, as well as our spiritual sense, to rightly judge these situations.

Don't second-guess yourself when you have a sense that something is wrong. Get up, get out, and stay away from it—no matter who may say differently.

PRAYER

Father, we come to You by the power invested in us by the name and blood of Jesus. We ask You for forgiveness for any involvement with the practice of necromancy and any related activity. Please cleanse our bodies, minds, spirits, homes, property, and loved ones of all residue of that practice, by the power of the blood of the Lamb. Thank You for the blood of Jesus, the truth of Your Word, and Your Holy Spirit. Lord, please give to us wisdom, discernment, and the courage to stand up for the truth and to depart from what is wrong. Cause us to hunger for Your truth. Manifest Your true signs, wonders, and miracles. We will be sure to give to You all the praise, honor, and glory. In Jesus's name, amen.

18

DISCERNING BETWEEN ANGELIC AND DEMONIC ACTIVITY

God created everything and everyone. (See Revelation 4:11.) Every power and every person that exists originated from Him. *"For by Him all things were created that are in heaven and that are on earth, visible and invisible, whether thrones or dominions or principalities or powers. All things were created through Him and for Him"* (Colossians 1:16).

There are holy, unfallen angels of God; there are also fallen, demonic angels. We are never to worship or bring attention to either type. A heaven-sent angel of the Lord would never want us to do that, anyhow.

Not all the angels that God made remained true to Him. Lucifer sat in heaven and saw all that God had created yet thought of himself as being greater. The power given to him went to his head. Although he may have been given *some* power, he soon found out that God *is* power. Because of his arrogance, God cast Lucifer out of heaven into hell. (See Isaiah 14:12–15.) He also evicted from heaven the angels who sided with Lucifer. (See Jude 1:6.)

Why Talk About Angels?

It's important to discuss angels along with the prophetic because angels are God's ministering messengers. (See Hebrews 1:14.) Jesus said that He sends His angels to testify to us in the church. (See Revelation 22:16.)

There have been times when I was aware of the presence and help of angels while prophesying over someone. I've also gone through particularly difficult seasons of life when I sensed that God had sent an angel to minister comfort to me. Other times, I've been in danger, and God has dispatched an angel to help me.

Angels are real. They are called to do God's bidding (see Psalm 103:20 NIV) and to guard and protect those who belong to Him (see Revelation 14:6).

God's angels also protect children. Jesus said to His disciples, *"Take heed that you do not despise one of these little ones, for I say to you that in heaven their angels always see the face of My Father who is in heaven"* (Matthew 18:10).

When the Lord sees a need that humans are not meeting, He may send an angel to help, as He did for the Israelites when they were hungry in the wilderness: *"Men ate angels' food; He sent them food to the full"* (Psalm 78:25).

Angels of God can preach the gospel (see Revelation 14:6), and they rejoice whenever a sinner repents. (See Luke 15:10.) We are not to worship angels; rather, angels lead us to worship the Lord. (See Colossians 2:18; Revelation 5:11–12.)

What's It Like to See an Angel?

Job described his angelic encounter this way: *"A spirit passed before my face; the hair on my body stood up. It stood still, but I could not discern its appearance. A form was before my eyes; there was silence; then I heard a voice…"* (Job 4:15–16).

When Mary Magdalene stood outside Jesus's tomb, crying, she stated that she had seen two angels in white, seated where Jesus's body had been—one at the head and the other at the foot. (See John 20:11–12.)

When Jesus returns to gather all believers, God's angels will accompany Him (see Matthew 16:27), and we'll all find out in person what they look like. They will gather His elect from one end of the heavens to the other. (See Matthew 24:31.)

Personal Accounts of Angelic Encounters

Whenever I've had experiences with angels, I've seen them in human appearance.

One day, my car broke down in the middle of the road in heavy traffic. A small red car pulled up behind me, and a man got out and started directing traffic around my stalled vehicle, all the while speaking to me in a way that calmed me. As soon as the tow truck arrived, he said, "They will take care of you now," and he walked toward the back of my car. Poof! He and the little red car disappeared. Without a doubt, an angel had appeared to help in my time of need.

Another time, I was on a ministry trip when a terrible storm began right when I was to check in to my hotel. I hurried to the side entrance, arms loaded, leading my two dogs on their leashes. I tried to stretch my arm past everything I was carrying to use the key card to open the door. Out of nowhere, a hand reached over me and opened the door. I walked inside, then turned to thank the individual who had helped me but saw no one. Thank God for angelic help!

I was driving in Florida and turned left into a shopping center when someone T-boned my van, striking the front passenger door. The front driver's side slammed into a tree, and I was badly injured. An ambulance transported me to a local hospital, where a police officer soon came to question me. He asked about the other passenger in my van. I said told him I'd been driving alone. He argued, "Many witnesses said someone got out of the front passenger seat and walked around the car until the ambulance arrived, then vanished." I started crying. "That must have been an angel," I said, "because that door is where the other vehicle hit me. No one could have opened it because it's demolished." The policeman's eyes grew wide as he remembered seeing that the door had been destroyed. Choked up, he said, "Yes, ma'am, I believe it."

You've Seen Angels Too

God hasn't left you out. He's no respecter of persons. (See Acts 10:34 KJV.) I guarantee that He has sent angels to help you at one time or another, whether or not you realized it at the time.

We need to be aware of how we treat strangers, for the Word admonishes us, *"Do not forget to show hospitality to strangers, for by so doing some people have shown hospitality to angels without knowing it"* (Hebrews 13:2 NIV).

We also need to beware of false reports of angelic visitations. The Internet is rife with postings of stories about angelic visitations, but God has given us this warning in His Word:

> Do not let anyone who delights in false humility and the worship of angels disqualify you. Such a person also goes into great detail about what they have seen; they are puffed up with idle notions by their unspiritual mind. (Colossians 2:18 NIV)

The Demonic Realm

Even though Jesus has defeated the demonic realm and made an open spectacle of it (see Colossians 2:15), demons exist and still torment Christian believers. Many times, we go through scary, demonic experiences because we have opened a door to the enemy through sin or by dabbling in something related to the occult, such as using an Ouija board or tarot cards, or seeking advice from a fortune-teller or a medium.

My family always attended church, but we had some terrifying demonic visitations because of things we were practicing in ignorance. I shared earlier about the havoc that was wreaked on our home due to the presence of an Ouija board. We would have haunted-house experiences of seeing dishes flying out of the cupboards, hearing footsteps in the hallways, having doors unlock themselves and blow open, and feeling the touch of a cold hand. Prolific nightmares were a constant event. We would move into a new home and think all was well, and then the terror would start up again. Poltergeists—mischievous demonic spirits—love to frighten unsuspecting victims.

Later on, when I had children of my own, I learned the error of our ways and was delivered from those wrongful practices. Because we kept our home and lives free from such things, my children and I were spared that kind of terror.

There are certain items that are considered by various traditions to bring good luck, such as the four-leaf clover (Irish tradition) and the Buona Fortuna charm (Italian tradition). Many people check their daily horoscope reading religiously, or make a habit of calling psychic hotlines. Some dabble in satanic cults, with witches and witchcraft; others follow the New Age movement. All these practices are considered part of the occult, and they result in the same curses.

In the book of Acts, we read, *"Many of those who had practiced magic brought their books together and burned them in the sight of all. And they counted up the value of them, and it totaled fifty thousand pieces of silver"* (Acts 19:19). The people burned the books of spells and enchantments when they learned the truth. That's what I did with any item I had in my possession that was related to the occult, including horoscopes and good-luck charms such as horseshoes and rabbits' feet. When you really think about it, how could a rabbit's foot be lucky? The rabbit from which it came certainly wasn't lucky!

Do you want to know why it is that you'll hear some accurate things spoken by psychics on those fortune-telling hotlines? It comes down to the Internet—specifically, social media. Once a psychic has you on the line, he or she can use your name and phone number to access untold information about you. The goal is to feed you just enough information to whet your appetite for more, so that you'll remain on the line and/or call back again. The longer you stay on the phone, the more you'll pay. Making money is the psychic's motive, and you're the sucker.

THE DEVIL'S "RESOURCES" OFTEN INCLUDE THE INTERNET AND SOCIAL MEDIA, ALONG WITH THE PRACTICE OF TAPPING INTO FAMILIAR SPIRITS.

John 8:44 says that Satan was *"a murderer from the beginning, and does not stand in the truth, because there is no truth in him. When he speaks a lie, he speaks from his own resources, for he is a liar and the father of it."*

The devil's "resources" often include the Internet and social media, along with the practice of tapping into familiar spirits.

The Good News

The good news is that there is deliverance and help to find freedom. Once you are loosed from bondage, you will have a testimony that you will be able to use to help deliver others and set them free.

It never shocks me to discover that an extremely gifted prophetic person had been trapped in some of the above practices, or even in a satanic cult. Leaders of those practices try to capitalize on the ignorance of an untrained prophetic person who is drawn to the supernatural. But we want the God kind of supernatural, not the devil's.

If you would like further information on obtaining release from any of the above, I would encourage you to read just about any title by Derek Prince. His books and teaching materials are timeless tools of priceless value that have helped to liberate many people from the devil's snares.

Translation

Translation is the spiritual experience of being translated or transported supernaturally by God from one spot to the next. This experience does not occur by the will of mere man but only according to the will of God.

The prophet Elijah was frequently translated. (See 1 Kings 18:10–12.) At the end of his life, God sent a chariot to transport him to heaven. (See 2 Kings 2:12.)

In John 6:16–21, the disciples were in a boat when Jesus walked across the water to join them. When they received Him into the boat, immediately they were transported to their destination.

In Acts 8:38–40, the Spirit of the Lord snatched Philip away to another land.

Jesus promises us that anyone who believes in Him will do the same works as He did, and even greater works, as well. (See John 14:12.)

Let me now share some personal examples with translation. For several years, I lived in Erie, Pennsylvania, where the winters see heavy snowfall.

One year, my friend Karen and her family planned a trip to her mother's in Aliquippa, near Pittsburgh, for Thanksgiving, and they invited me and my two children to join them. We decided to leave early in the morning because the news stations were warning of the approach of a nasty blizzard.

We were halfway to Aliquippa when the storm hit. It would have taken us just as long to go back to Erie as it would take to continue to our destination, so we pressed on. Suddenly, a tractor trailer on the road in front of us jackknifed.

"What do I do?" Karen screamed.

"Turn into the area where you have the most room to stop!" I shouted back. Then I covered my eyes so I wouldn't see us crash.

"Joni, look!" Karen shouted.

I uncovered my eyes and saw nothing in the road in front of us.

"Look behind us!" Karen exclaimed.

At first, I thought perhaps the truck's cab had detached from the trailer and that we had driven through the opening. However, when I turned my head and looked back, I saw the jackknifed tractor trailer across the road far behind us. God had protected and transported us and our children about a mile down the road.

Another time, my friend Carol and I traveled from Charlotte, North Carolina, to a Bible study in Moravian Falls. Torrential rain was coming down, and I grew nervous as Carol kept riding the middle line. Suddenly, a car rounded the mountain curve and came at us head-on, only it didn't hit us. We passed through it as if our car and we ourselves were not made of solid material. We saw everything that was in the other car, including the trunk, on our journey through it to the other side. The sound and sensation were that of being sucked through the hose of a vacuum cleaner. Carol and I were both in shock after being "spit out" the other end. As Christians, we glorified God, but we also wondered what the people in the other car were thinking. At our Bible study, we testified about our miracle.

On yet another occasion, I was alone at home one Saturday, and during an extended time of serious prayer, I cried out, "I just want to see Your face, Jesus!"

An open vision suddenly occurred in which I saw the face of a man from India. The man was wearing a turban. In an audible voice, the Lord said, "*My face is* the face of My people."

Instantly, I became whisked through a tunnel, and I landed on a dirt street in a foreign land I knew to be India. I saw a man being crowded by a large group of people wanting him to pray for them. The people trampled one another in their efforts to reach the man. An angel of the Lord directed me to help organize the crowd so that everyone remained safe. The experience seemed to last for hours.

As suddenly as I'd left home, I landed on the floor of my living room. I was unsettled, wondering how long I'd been gone.

At the time, I worked at Derek Prince Ministries, where we started every workday with staff devotions. Our phone system had an answering machine, but if a caller knew the extension of the person he or she wanted to reach, there was the option of calling a person's desk directly.

When I arrived at work on Monday morning, I quickly stopped by my desk to drop off my purse before going to devotions. As I did so, my phone rang. The caller turned out to be a good friend of the ministry at CBN. He said, "I knew if anyone would answer their phone, you would!" He then began to relate to me that he had been in India over the weekend. He talked about a large crowd and said that a woman had suddenly showed up and helped organize the people. Astonished, I fell into my chair and told him, "I know. It was me. I was there. I'm the one who helped you." We shared other details and quickly realized that God had translated me to India on Saturday to help.

Astral Projection

Astral projection is a practice that belongs to the realms of divination and witchcraft. Defined as "the ability of a person's spirit to travel to distant places," it is also known as teleportation, or "the act or process of moving an object or person by psychokinesis"—which, in the world of literary fiction, means "instantaneous travel between two locations without crossing the intervening space." Telekinesis is defined as "the production of motion in objects (as by a spiritualistic medium) without contact or other physical means."

I ministered a few times at a church where the pastor told tall tales, made false accusations, and displayed severe temper tantrums.

Everything came to a head when he had an extreme outburst one Sunday morning. He exhibited extreme paranoia and screamed at the people that he had physically projected himself into some of their bedrooms and had heard their accusations about him. The congregants were terrified when he threatened to show up in their bedrooms again if they said anything else against him.

I ministered at a regional women's meeting in a large city in the South. I discerned that a woman on their board dabbled in a type of dangerous teaching. As I struck up a conversation with her, I prayed under my breath for the Spirit of truth to reveal the truth from her own mouth, and He did. She had been attending a school for extrasensory perception (ESP) and clairvoyance in which she was learning such techniques as astral projection. She and several of the other ladies laughed as she related how she had "freaked them out" by showing up in their homes for practice. They seemed to have no idea that Christians should not do such things. Our discussion ended up being a time of teaching during which I was able to help bring them back into proper alignment with the Word.

The Bible teaches many things that modern-day churches don't, such as prophecy, healing, deliverance, and so forth. Jesus is the same yesterday, today, and forever. (See Hebrews 13:8.) His power hasn't diminished; rather, it has increased because He has empowered the church to do the same works and even greater works, too. (See John 14:12.)

It is imperative that we use the Word of God as our plumb line so that we tap into God's realms of spiritual power and authority rather than engage in counterfeit, demonic activity.

PRAYER

Dear Lord, thank You for Your Word, Your Son, Your Holy Spirit, Your angels, and Your power. May we walk in Your will and ways, and please You with the lives You've given to us. Let us never turn to the counterfeit but always seek what is of You. In Jesus's name, amen.

19

DETECTING THE SPIRIT
OF JEZEBEL

We must beware of the spirit of Jezebel—a subtle, sneaky, controlling spirit of manipulation that particularly hates and seeks to destroy the prophetic so that she, Jezebel, will not be "found out." The spirit of Jezebel is in constant battle against the spirit of Elijah, which, by contrast, seeks to edify, exhort, and encourage.

Although named for a female queen (see 1 Kings 16:30–31), the Jezebel spirit is not gender specific; it can operate through males and females alike. However, for the purpose of greater clarity in this chapter, I will refer to this spirit using female pronouns.

Women are the best judges of other women, just as men are the best judges of their fellow men. A man will sense a player a mile away, while many women are enamored of such men and their charming ways. In the same way, men are often oblivious to the operation of a Jezebel in their midst. No matter how blatant it may appear to the women nearby, most men will be so bewitched by a Jezebel that they will defend her, even to their own wife.

In most cases, a female Jezebel hates other women—especially those who are exceptionally discerning, for they represent a threat to her domain. Therefore, she will do everything in her power to discredit and destroy them. She may accuse them of making up falsehoods, argue that they don't belong in positions of leadership, question whether they really hear from God, and so forth. A Jezebel's witchcraft extends into the spiritual realm, possibly causing other women to feel as if they are crazy, unintelligent, worthless, and a host of other condemnations. Her onslaught often causes her victims to experience extreme warfare in their marriage or in their relationship with church leaders; it may also lead to depression and thoughts of suicide. A Jezebel endeavors to bring on those who oppose her every manner of illness, accident, and calamity—even death.

Jezebel will appear to most men as sincere, caring, and intelligent. She will lead them to believe that the women who recognize her for who she is are simply envious and "out to get her." All the while, her evil spiritual tentacles are driven deeper into the souls of the men she seduces, so that any accusations raised against her prompt her male victims to defend her all the more strongly. She is a master of seduction; her deception operates at a high level, and her goal is to divide and conquer.

The entire time a Jezebel cozies up to her victim, she is planning his demise. She discovers his weaknesses and capitalizes on them through flattery and actions that appear to serve him.

Quite often, Jezebel will take a position in the church where it seems she is filling a role that no one else wants. She may even take on multiple tasks. Part of her controlling strategy is to make herself indispensable. She strives to always appear as the kind, caring, anointed woman of which others are jealous. She may even put on an act of being "poor, misunderstood, and misjudged me," and may cry if confronted.

She will especially seek to invade the area of intercession, where she will "wow" others with her intuition and information, using these to control and manipulate other intercessors as well as the church pastors and leadership. By gaining control of the intercession, she becomes queen of charismatic witchcraft with her seemingly intense personal knowledge, which is actually the way in which she gains others' agreement with the verbal curses she prays. Those who oppose her will begin to experience illness and mishaps and are likely to make a hasty departure from the group, if not the church altogether.

Jezebel is a guided missile sent by the enemy to destroy her target, which is usually a man in a high level of authority.

There are times when Jezebel may even deceive other women in order to recruit them into her camp to do her bidding and help her accomplish her dirty work. But make no mistake about it: The Jezebel apprentices-in-training will know she is the boss. Even when they realize what she is doing, they will continue to fear and obey her because they perceive their weakness compared to her strength. This tactic may serve to further confuse her male victims, because the support of other women will often lead men to believe she is okay, merely misunderstood by the discerning women who voice warnings about her.

A JEZEBEL ENDEAVORS TO BRING ON THOSE WHO OPPOSE HER EVERY MANNER OF ILLNESS, ACCIDENT, AND CALAMITY—EVEN DEATH.

In private situations with her victims, Jezebel appears vulnerable and compliant, thereby gaining further trust and favor, all the while injecting her venom. She isn't necessarily after a position of power for herself, as long as she can be the "power behind the throne."

She may even use subtle seduction by wearing certain types of clothing or applying certain scents of perfume. She will act as a servant, possibly by serving coffee or baking cookies for the man she is targeting. She will pay close attention to his personal needs, the sports teams he follows, his personal likes and dislikes, and so forth. After a while, he will feel as if she understands him better than anyone else—never realizing it is because she has studied and learned his ways in order to manipulate him! She will be ever so conscious and mindful of any way in which she may slide another tentacle into place.

All the while, the man's wife, and other women, see through her plan and try to warn the man. Eventually, other men may even notice the warning signs and sound an alert. But, by this point, it may be too late. Bewitched by her charms, her victim defends her all the more whenever someone issues a warning.

Drama is the calling card of the Jezebel spirit. Jezebel craves attention and power at any cost, good or bad. Embellishment and outright lies go right along with her quest for power, and destruction always litters her path.

So, how does one go about unseating the Jezebel spirit? By starving her, cutting off the information and attention she craves. If you desire to disempower a Jezebel, start by removing her from any positions of authority she occupies. Take her out of any information loop. And pray, for prayer is always your greatest weapon. Pray for God to open the eyes and ears of her victims. Pray for God Himself to put a Holy-Ghost restraining order on her. Pray for the Spirit of truth to reveal and expose even the hidden agendas in a way that no one could deny. Pray Psalm 35 out loud. Plead the blood of Jesus over the mind, body, spirit, and life of her victims and their loved ones.

If you must publicly expose a Jezebel to the church congregation, expect a hellish onslaught—even a divided church. But do not back down or give up. God is not pleased when we allow Jezebel to have control. It is certainly better to "drain the swamp" and please God than to please Jezebel and those who choose to be deceived by her. God says in the book of Revelation, "*Nevertheless I have a few things against you, because you allow that woman Jezebel, who calls herself a prophetess, to teach and seduce My servants...*" (Revelation 2:20).

There are no diplomatic options available when it comes to dealing with Jezebel. There's no use in trying to reason, argue, or play a blame game with that spirit. All such things are a waste of time and energy, not to mention that they will feed her need for attention. Once her authority and feeding lines have been shut down, it will drive her crazy, and she will begin to manifest her true colors so blatantly that all will see the truth, including her victims.

Jezebel is a sociopathic spirit that has no fear of either God or man. Don't ignore what your discernment tells you. Cover yourself with the blood of Jesus. Trust God, and He will unseat Jezebel as you and others pray and refuse to back down or play her games.

How Ahab Fits In

If a Jezebel marries, it will be to a weak, submissive man—like Ahab, who was the husband of the original Jezebel in the Bible. (See 1 Kings 16:30–31.) Even married, Jezebel will still try to spiritually seduce her church pastor or other men in power.

Ahab is passively compliant on the surface, always defending his Jezebel and meekly carrying out her will as an obliging servant. All the while, inside, he is raging with passive-aggressive anger because she has emasculated him. In his mind, he will get back at the Jezebel he serves by taking out his anger on others, thinking that such behavior makes him manly. He will seem gentle and reachable, but—have no doubts about it— as her willing slave, he is every bit as evil and as dangerous as Jezebel.

A MAN WHO ALLOWS HIMSELF TO BECOME EMASCULATED BY AN EVIL WOMAN LIKE JEZEBEL EITHER FADES INTO A CORNER AND BECOMES INVISIBLE OR BECOMES ANGRY, BITTER, AND DANGEROUS.

A man who allows himself to become emasculated by an evil woman like Jezebel either fades into a corner and becomes invisible or becomes angry, bitter, and dangerous. The original Ahab in the Bible sold his soul and became evil. *"There was no one like Ahab who sold himself to do wickedness in the sight of the LORD, because Jezebel his wife stirred him up"* (1 Kings 21:25).

By the way, not every man whom Jezebel targets necessarily becomes an Ahab. Case in point, the prophet Elijah. Jezebel may bewitch certain men with her spells for a time, but when the veil is lifted, they vehemently denounce her.

A Sobering Story

Years ago, I traveled to a different city to participate in a prophetic ministry weekend. The leadership team consisted of five businessmen, and the intercessory component was led by a very wealthy woman with a stately home of great extravagance. In a side room she referred to as the "Prophets' Quarters," she had hosted many visiting ministers.

Even after her husband left her for another woman, this woman continued to extend hospitality to guest speakers brought in by this prophetic group, as well as hosted the businessmen for their own meetings. Many mornings, these five men would meet at her home to pray together and discuss their day while she served them coffee and breakfast.

Everyone else seemed taken in by this woman and expressed great admiration of her, but I felt a check in my spirit that made me more than a bit skeptical. However, the men praised her and told me how she had ministered to them and to the various guest speakers she hosted. They said she often gave confirmation to them about things she "couldn't possibly have known anything about."

One particular day, I met individually with all five of the men and their spouses for a time of personal prophetic ministry. After that, I headed directly for the evening meeting at the ministry facility.

I returned to the mansion that night feeling exhausted. As I went inside, I was startled by the lady of the house standing up from where she'd been sitting on a bench in the dark front hallway. She had waited up for me with a snack plate and a glass of tea. In spite of my fatigue, I thanked her and sat down with her.

She hadn't been able to attend that night's meeting because of a school of event for one of her children, so she asked me how everything had gone, and we discussed it a bit. Then, out of the blue, she said that one of the five businessmen had called her and had excitedly told her about the prophetic time he and his wife had had with me that afternoon. She said he'd given me permission to tell her all about it, as he hadn't had time to discuss it with her in detail.

Something about her claim didn't ring true for me. I said, "I'm sorry. I'm so tired, I'm afraid I didn't catch all of what you just said. Can you please repeat that?"

She repeated it, exactly the way I thought she'd said it.

Again, I felt an uneasy check in my spirit. So, I simply said, "I doubt I'd remember it all right now. Can we revisit this discussion tomorrow at lunch? I'm exhausted and need to get some rest." Then I went to my room.

I sat on the side of the bed a while, then finally decided to call the man she'd mentioned and ask him if he really wanted me to share his private information with her. As I reached for the bedside phone, the Lord put a hand on mine to stop me, and I heard Him say, "Don't do it!"

I asked, "Why?"

He said, "Pull down the top of the bed."

I replied, "What? Why?"

He said, "Just do it!"

I reached up and pulled back the covers and the pillow.

"Not like that," He said. "Stand up and pull the top of the bed back, out from the wall."

Never in my life would I have expected what I saw. There sat a baby monitor. It was turned on. Clearly, the lady of the house had put it there to monitor what was said in that room. The names of well-known ministry leaders and their wives who had stayed in that room flashed in my mind. I sat motionless and in shock at the implications. That woman had heard everything that had been said and done. I felt sickened.

The Lord had me unplug the monitor. The next thing I heard was the woman stomping across the floor upstairs as she ran to shut off the alarm that rang on her end of the monitor as a result.

The Lord then told me to take my shower, then lay out a set of clothes and be ready to leave the house early the next morning. He instructed me to go to a nearby donut shop, where I was to call the ministry board member the woman had spoken of and ask him to meet me there so that I could question him and also share with him what I'd discovered.

Over the course of that weekend, I discovered even more. The woman had also positioned a baby monitor in the decorative centerpiece on a table in the room where the businessmen routinely met. So much for her ability to tell them about things she "couldn't possibly have known anything about."

The businessmen had long referred to this woman as the leader of their private intercessory team. This woman, with the aid of two female cohorts, had convinced the men to confide in them rather than in their own wives. She had even begun turning one man against his own wife, telling him that he needed to have her committed to an insane asylum and then divorce her. Evidently, she had designs to marry that man, since her own husband had left her.

These five businessmen had become puppets, controlled and manipulated by a queen Jezebel and two Jezebels-in-training. The entire ministry folded a couple of years later, and God crumbled the kingdom of that particular Jezebel.

Deliverance of a Jezebel

In later years, I led ministry teams composed of twenty-two women around the nation for Women's Prophetic Destiny conferences. God gave me a schedule to follow, and I brought along various women to teach on their particular area of expertise related to prophetic ministry: dreams and visions; prophetic dance; prophetic deliverance; prophetic songs of the Lord; writing; women in business; and so forth.

At a church in Florida, I concluded one of my teaching sessions—a session that dealt with the Jezebel spirit—with a time when the women in attendance could receive prayer from whichever teacher was anointed in the area in which they desired impartation. Because I strongly believe that I am to open the doors for others that God opens for me, I encouraged the women traveling with me to bring along any women they happened to be mentoring. One of my team members had brought with her a woman who fit the description of a Jezebel. Wouldn't you know, she approached me for prayer.

"So, do you think I have a Jezebel spirit?" she asked me.

I said, "Do you think that you do?"

"Well, your teaching totally described me," she replied.

"So, what do you want to do about it?"

"Cast it out of me!" she said, throwing her hands up.

"I can't," I replied. "You invited it in, so, if you are serious, you have to evict it." I then told her to go to the altar and renounce or evict everything she could think of I had taught on that resonated with her. I told her she should next ask the Lord to cleanse her with the blood of Jesus and ask the Holy Spirit to enter into every one of those areas instead. I let her know I would be there to help, if needed.

She followed my instructions and experienced a dramatic deliverance. After that, she continued traveling with our team and made valuable contributions to our work.

A Word of Hope

There is hope for anyone who wants it. Even someone wrapped in the Jezebel spirit can be delivered. God is the God of miracles. Please do not use this teaching as an excuse to discredit and destroy anyone; let's destroy, not succumb to, the activity of that spirit, knowing that there is hope for anyone who truly wants deliverance.

Additionally, let's not falsely accuse a woman or a man of operating in the Jezebel spirit just because he or she has a strong personality. Let's be truly discerning about this area.

PRAYER

Dear Lord, thank You for the blood of Jesus. We ask that it would cover and protect us and our loved ones from the spirit of Jezebel and all evil spirits. Please don't allow us or our loved ones to be deceived or bewitched. Give us the wisdom and ability to discern and rightly handle any situations that may arise. In Jesus's name, amen.

20

HOUSEKEEPING HINTS FOR PROPHETIC MINISTRY

As you pursue this prophetic journey you've begun, it becomes more exciting every day. It's always an adventure.

Don't give up when you don't see your promises fulfilled right away. Some things happen immediately, while other things may take 20 or more years. Through it all, we learn and grow in God, as well as in our personal lives and our ability to persevere. To everything, there is a time and a season, and God knows the right time and place for each word to be fulfilled.

The hardest thing to endure is seeing those we love waste time. But we must maintain our faith and trust in God that He will work it all out in the best possible way.

Sometimes, God's voice seems easy to hear; other times, He seems far away or even silent. We still need to trust in His love and goodness while we wait for His response.

God may vary the way He speaks to us. One day, He may speak in visions; the next day, He may speak in a dream; still the next, He may communicate in a still, small voice. Allow Him to draw you deeper into love with Him, and further into His will, as He woos you in this way.

Be Ready to Brave Trials, Tribulations, and Trying Situations

The prophetic isn't always neat and tidy. Quite often, a prophetic person will have a life that is used as an object lesson. We prophetic people may experience certain hardships before the rest of the body of Christ so that we can forewarn them and/or help them handle the experience when it happens to them. In the meantime, we become subject to the ridicule and condemnation of those who suppose that our trials are a form of punishment for some secret wrongs in our lives.

A prophetic church will often attract "strange" people. Some are truly prophetic, others are demonic, and others are simply a bit "off." The supernatural fascinates people of all kinds, drawing them in. Even witches are attracted to the power they sense coming from a prophetic group. Just because it doesn't come in a neat package with a nice bow on it doesn't mean we should reject it, only that we need to have true watchmen in place who can sniff out and properly discern the real from the fake. We also need leaders who are not afraid to stand up and stop the fake in its tracks.

When you work as an itinerant prophetic minister, your presence will stir up the atmosphere of the area where you are ministering. Crazy weather and even earthquakes may occur as a result. People may manifest unusual behaviors and odd reactions. Stuff happens when the prophetic anointing appears.

Sometimes, you just need to "hit and run." There have been times when the Lord has told me to get out of town under the cover of darkness after a meeting so that I might avoid serious repercussions—not because I had done anything wrong, but because He had used me to turn some things around, which always ruffles someone's feathers.

THERE MAY BE TIMES WHEN PEOPLE SET THEMSELVES AGAINST YOU WELL BEFORE YOUR ARRIVAL, ALL BECAUSE OF THEIR PAST EXPOSURE TO ERRANT TEACHINGS AND POOR EXAMPLES OF PROPHETIC MINISTRY.

I've been followed from one town to the next by tornadic storms that no meteorologist had predicted. God will keep us safe; we just need to obey Him when He says to get in our car and go.

There may be times when people set themselves against you well before your arrival, all because of their past exposure to errant teachings and poor examples of prophetic ministry. When this occurs, you will sense it, but you cannot afford to let it taint the ministry you are called to do.

Advice for Interpersonal Relations

It can be difficult to find friends who will let you just be you. Many people will expect you to be "on" at all times and ready to prophesy at the drop of a hat. They will sometimes treat you oddly because they fear you can read their every thought and know their every move.

When you travel, whether you are staying in a home or a hotel, be prepared for frequent invasions of your privacy. Your host may bring to you just about everyone he or she knows, hoping you will give them all a word. Other times, you may have to battle through the junk someone is dealing with, even as you try to prepare for a meeting. In all these events, obey God, for it just may be that He has strategically positioned you in the home of someone whose life you will save by speaking into it.

Case in point: One time, a woman graciously invited me to stay in her home when I discovered that the local hotel was completely booked. The woman's husband begrudgingly agreed to let me stay. That night, the Lord revealed to me that this man intended to kill his wife. I cautiously relayed this information to the woman the next morning. As a munitions expert, her husband had arranged a gas leak with a curbside trigger. I had his wife call the gas company, and they confirmed this detail. Praise God, this woman was able to get out alive.

Another time, I was scheduled to stay in a motel. When I found out that my host family had had their electricity shut off and had no food in the house, I canceled my motel reservation in order to give them the money that would have been used on the room to cover their electric bill and the purchase of some groceries. For the remainder of my time in their town, I stayed in their home and showed God's love to them.

Relationships can be difficult because of your ability to discern certain things that others cannot. Whether this skill is a saving grace or a source of heartache, thank God for the privilege of exercising it for His glory.

A Prophet's Budget

It's important to keep your living expenses to a minimum if you feel called to a prophetic walk of faith. Don't rent the most expensive apartment or drive a vehicle with huge monthly payments. Other people are unlikely to anticipate your travel expenses, let alone your day-to-day cost of living. Therefore, you must keep your expenses low enough that you won't have to make decisions in ministry that are based on your bank account. You can't have your mind on those things if you want to hear clearly from God. You must give yourself the freedom to keep your mind on things above. (See Colossians 3:2.)

―――――――――――――――

THE WALK OF A PROPHETIC PERSON IS
RARELY EASY OR UNCOMPLICATED.
WE MUST BE WILLING TO PAY THE PRICE OF
BEING AN OVERCOMER, OR ELSE WE NEED TO
DUMB DOWN, QUIT, AND NOT WALK IN OUR
CALLING AT ALL.

―――――――――――――――

The walk of a prophetic person is rarely easy or uncomplicated. We must be willing to pay the price of being an overcomer, or else we need to dumb down, quit, and not walk in our calling at all. But we who are called to this life love adventure too much to do that, don't we?

If we want to walk this thing out to completion, we need to get totally on board with it and learn as much as we can about it. We must study to show ourselves *"approved to God"* (2 Timothy 2:15). We must seek to walk it out in the love and heart of God, not any personal agenda. And we must choose to go forward and never look back.

Burdens You Must Bear

There may be times when a simple restaurant setting will seem so loud to you that you want to run out screaming. It's due to the supernatural noise, not the natural sounds.

There will be occasions when a prophetic wave of sorrow or fear will overtake you to such a degree that you can barely handle it, let alone sleep. We need to learn to discern and handle such occasions, just as nurses and doctors must learn to handle sickness and death. We can't feel personally responsible for whether a person walks things out in a right way or turns from the Lord.

You can warn people about the danger of oncoming storms, whether natural or spiritual, until you are blue in the face; but if they want to stay put and be terrorized and risk ending up dying, it's not your fault.

You may see the sorrow up ahead for someone who chooses a wrong mate, but that person is the one who ultimately must make the choice and live with it. All you can do is speak your words of warning, then pray.

You may see in the spirit that a friend's spouse is being unfaithful; but if you try to tell your friend without providing irrefutable proof, your friend will label you as jealous.

Even if God uses you to give someone a final opportunity to make necessary changes, and that person still blows it, you must pick yourself up, dust yourself off, and move forward. You are not responsible for anyone's response. The times when someone lights up at our words and makes drastic changes when God conveys His heart through us makes it all worthwhile.

I'll never forget the time I ministered at the House of David church in Nashville, Tennessee. After the service, I discovered that a man in the congregation who didn't speak English had heard every word I said in his own language. The Holy Spirit had interpreted for him. God is still the God of miracles.

CONCLUSION:
STEP INTO YOUR GIFT

It's unfathomable to me, in this day and time, how some Christians do not believe that God still speaks to us. Most Christians agree that they are supposed to pray, but far fewer believe they can hear God speak. Why pray to a God we don't expect to answer us?

Hebrews 2:4 says, *"God also bearing witness both with signs and wonders, with various miracles, and gifts of the Holy Spirit, according to His own will...."*

So, how will He speak? Any way He chooses—*"according to His own will."* He is, after all, God. Let us not put Him in a box. He can speak through nature, the Word, songs, movies, "picture" visions, "video" types of visions/visitations/dreams, "fleeting thoughts," impressions, billboard signs, comments made by others...the list is endless. He will surely use you, me, and anything or anyone else He may choose to use. If we don't put Him in a box, we won't be putting ourselves and our futures in a box—and life will be a very exciting adventure for us, indeed.

It is the same Holy Spirit in us all. Not an older, smarter, or "better" one—so let Him use *you*, no matter your age, status in life, or condition.

God made you to be who you are. He gave you the prophetic gift you have. He designed you to be observant, alert, and perceptive. You see things others don't see because that's how God designed you. You've received favor that others haven't because God has crowned you with it. At the same time, you've been through warfare that is almost unfathomable because the enemy hates you.

Welcome to the club, my prophetic friend.

God's supernatural, divine enablement in our lives often takes place as the result of the seed of a prophetic word. It changes hearts and lives in a real way. When we are used in that way, it has a tendency to stir things up—even people. Don't be surprised by it. Let it be a sign unto you that you are on the right track.

Don't be afraid to step out further than you've ever stepped out before. You have what it takes, so use those giftings and abilities. Someone may be fading fast, in need of the spark of hope and encouragement that you alone can deliver. Do it!

I pray for a supernatural impartation of expectation for you as you go forward in your quest for more of God. I believe you will see and experience the fulfillment of God's promises as you pursue Him.

Nothing is too big for God, so dream big! When your vision becomes greater than your abilities and knowledge, the Holy Spirit Himself can mentor you.

It's time to rise and shine and let the glory of the Lord rise and shine on you. Gross darkness may encompass the earth, but His light and glory are yours to behold. (See Isaiah 60:1–2.)

IT'S TIME TO RISE AND SHINE AND
LET THE GLORY OF THE LORD RISE AND SHINE
ON YOU. GROSS DARKNESS MAY ENCOMPASS
THE EARTH, BUT HIS LIGHT AND GLORY ARE
YOURS TO BEHOLD.

You've been faithful to pray for and believe for others; now, it's time to believe for *you*, as well.

It's important to write the vision God places in your heart. (See Habakkuk 2:2–4.) Don't stray from or give up on it. Don't word curse it. Nurture it with prayers and declarations of faith. Act upon it. Walk it out. Achieve it.

Don't despise small beginnings. (See Zechariah 4:10 NLT.) If you dream of ministering in stadiums, as is done by such individuals as Benny Hinn or Reinhard Bonnke, you may need to start by being faithful to minister in a small home group. As you are faithful in the little, your dream will unfold into the much. Why would God entrust us with a huge stadium if we can't handle a smaller task?

Do your due diligence to learn all you can. Sit at the feet of and serve others, like Elisha did with Elijah. (See 1 Kings 19:19–21.) As you do, God will bless what you put your hands to do and will also send to you those who will help you.

Respect and honor those who are your leaders and teachers. To the degree that you do so, God will also do for you. Give honor to whom it is due, as Romans 13:7 admonishes us.

Don't seek to be like anyone but who God made you to be. You will reach people no one else can reach because of who you are.

Cultivate a compassionate heart, and don't let it become hardened by the spiritual warfare you experience or the attitudes and opinions of others. No one should be permitted to have that kind of power over you.

If you sense your heart growing cold, or your body getting tired, take time aside with the Lord and let Him restore you. Even Jesus had to separate Himself from the masses and recuperate from time to time. (See, for example, Luke 5:16.)

Maintain a teachable spirit. You will never know enough, let alone everything.

Give away what you learn. There's more where that came from. God has an endless supply.

Be humble. God rewards the humble and lifts them up. (See, for example, Psalm 147:6.)

Keep short accounts with God. Don't let the sun go down while you are separated from Him in any way.

Be strong and very courageous! Don't be afraid nor be dismayed, for the Lord your God is with you wherever you go! (See Joshua 1:9.)

Never, ever give up. Never.

PRAYER

Lord, thank You for Your Word, Your Son, Your Holy Spirit, and for allowing us to take part in what You are doing in the earth today. May we be found faithful and finish well. In Jesus's name, amen.

Addendum A:

GUIDELINES FOR PROPHETS AND PROPHETIC TEAMS, AND THOSE WHO RECEIVE THEM

If you are a pastor or the leader of a prophetic team, I encourage you to establish clear guidelines for those under your leadership. Post those guidelines somewhere people can see them, and be sure every member of your team has a printout or a digital copy of them, as well. This policy will reduce the number of misunderstandings.

Additionally, you should supply a sheet of guidelines to anyone receiving a prophetic word from you.

It is unfortunate, but many ministries have had to shut down the operation of prophetic ministry because of those who choose to operate in a controlling, manipulative way with it. If you establish and clearly make your guidelines known and enforce them, it will save you and your congregation a lot of trouble.

There are cases where people still ignore the guidelines, but if you have them, you have the plumb line with which to bring accountability. If necessary, you can then shut down a problematic person and remove them rather than shut down the entire ministry.

Following are two lists of guidelines: one for your team members, and one to give to those over whom you prophesy. Feel free to copy and post the chart and add your ministry information on it. Add to it or subtract from it as you feel led.

After that are some fun prophetic activations for your group to try out.

Enjoy your adventure in the prophetic! The best *is* yet to come!

Personal Prophetic Ministry Team Guidelines

You are serving on our prophetic ministry team because you have agreed to be accountable to our guidelines. We are thankful for your heart to love God's people and for your willingness to give of your time to participate in prophetic ministry. We appreciate your abiding by the following guidelines; otherwise, we will ask you to step down.

1. Pray and seek to get words of edification, exhortation, and comfort, per the Scriptures. (See 1 Corinthians 14:3.)

2. Make those to whom you prophesy comfortable, but hold conversation to a minimum. Do not let anyone tell you about themselves before you pray for them.

3. Make sure they have a way to record the word or a person to scribe for them. (If not, use your own phone and then send it to them.)

4. Pray in a clear, audible voice. Give the word in a mannerly fashion. No manifesting.

5. Stay out of the personal space of those over whom you prophesy. Do not engage in physical touch unless you have asked for and received permission to do so. If permission has been granted, touch only the shoulder, arm, or hand.

6. Have your Bible with you, and try to give a corresponding Scripture verse to back up whatever you say.

7. Ask God for "golden nuggets" that are specific to your recipients so that they will know the word is for them.

8. Do not offer medical advice or diagnoses, and never suggest that someone stop taking prescribed medication.

9. Never prophesy monetary donations to yourself or to anyone else.

10. Never engage in "matchmaking prophesy," nor respond to inquiries regarding dates or mates.

11. Never prophesy the sex of unborn babies.

12. Never prophesy moves to a certain ministry or across the country.

13. Never give predictions regarding life or death.

14. Never seek to communicate with the deceased, a practice that is contrary to the Scriptures.

15. Never prophesy correction. If you feel correction is needed, write out your concern in a note, along with your signature, the date, and your contact information. Then, give the note to your team leader.

Personal Prophetic Ministry Guidelines for Recipients

We have an established ministry team whose members are accountable to this ministry. If you choose to allow a stranger who is present to minister to you, we cannot be responsible for the outcome. We can only hold our own team members accountable. Our goal is to give words that match the Scriptures and bring forth edification, exhortation, and comfort.

Our teams are practicing hearing from God. They are volunteering to pray for you and to discover what they may receive. We pray that your time with us is a blessing. May God fulfill each and every promise you have been given.

1. We do not prophesy, nor do we respond to inquiries regarding, dates, mates, the sex of unborn babies, moves to this ministry or across the country, predictions regarding life or death, or communication with deceased loved ones—a practice that is contrary to the Scriptures.

2. We suggest that you record your word so that you may recall it accurately. You may choose to record the word using your phone or a digital recorder; or, you might ask a friend to act as scribe and write it down for you as you receive it.

3. Please do not tell any of our team members anything about yourself prior to or during prayer.

4. Please do not speak while someone is praying for you. If you have a question, you may ask it after the prayer has concluded. However, please do not request personal counsel regarding the word that was spoken.

5. We do not take questions regarding decisions you need to make. We are simply here to deliver to you what we hear from the Lord.

6. Please get up and leave the area as soon as your ministry time is over so that the team may have time to minister to all who desire to be prayed for.

7. We suggest that you write out your word as soon as you can so that you can better access, interpret, and pray over it.

8. Share your word with your pastor, your spouse, and/or an accountability partner.

9. Test your prophetic word according to the plumb line of God's Word. He will never advise you in any way that opposes it.

10. Never make major changes in your life based solely upon the prophecy you receive today. Seek the counsel of your pastor, church elders, and others you trust.

11. If you don't feel the word is for you, simply disregard it. "Chew up the meat and spit out the bones," as they say. Receive what you feel is accurate, and toss out what you feel might not be.

12. Know that a personal prophetic word is conditional upon your aligning yourself with and pursuing it. Understand that doing so is your own responsibility. No one else can do it for you.

Addendum B:

PERSONAL PROPHETIC MINISTRY ACTIVATIONS

The church has long taught *about* the Bible; Christians *say* they believe what's written in it, yet they are rarely *activated* by the church to do what it says they can do. Why would anyone want to attend a dead, dry church that doesn't operate in the power being preached about?

When the church is an alive and activated example of the Word of God, people will believe what we preach. Otherwise, we are no different from a fairy tale to the general public.

When the Azusa Street Revival happened, people came from all over the world to experience the power and presence of God. We shouldn't have to travel anywhere to get that. It should be a normal occurrence in every church.

However, if it isn't happening where you are, you shouldn't be afraid to go where it is.

Here are a few suggestions for those who want to practice their prophetic gift in order to effect change in the church and outside it, as well. We must exercise the gifts by using them. (See Romans 12:6.)

Musical Chairs

Set up some chairs in a circle, using one less chair than the number of people participating. (If there are six people, use five chairs.) Play music on the device of your choosing. When the music stops, whoever is left standing will either prophesy over the other people or will have them prophesy over him or her. Change it up each time until all everyone has had a turn.

Line Dance

This activity works well with about twenty people, but you may adjust it according to the number of people participating. It is similar to musical chairs.

Line up enough chairs for half the participants to sit down wearing blindfolds. Have the remaining participants stand in front of them, so that everyone is paired up.

When you start the music, those standing should start walking, making a circle around the chairs. When the music stops, those who are walking should stop in front of the nearest seated person and lightly touch that person's shoulder with the fingertip only. (No talking allowed by those who are standing up, to preserve anonymity!) The people who are seated must pray, prophesy, or sing over the person standing before them until the music starts again, at which point they must stop.

Each time the music stops, you should vary the length of time the prophesying occurs. The duration need not be long; thirty seconds, one minute, a minute and a half, and two minutes are acceptable.

After you have stopped the music five or six times, have everyone switch places so that those who were seated have a chance to walk around and be prophesied over. Try to make sure the folks sitting don't end up prophesying over the same person over and over.

Christmas Cards

Start your Christmas cards early and pray for a word for each person on your list. You can do this even if you are sending e-cards.

Local Churches

Make a list of the churches in your area and pray for each of them. Consider sending them a word in a little note card. Include a monetary offering if you feel so led.

Hot Seat

My friends and I love to surprise one another's houseguests by hosting dinners and putting our houseguests in the hot seat for prayer afterward.

Obviously, we try to make sure the person we choose is likely to be willing to receive prayer.

Shotgun

Bring two or three people up front and have them take turns calling out names of other individuals in the room to prophesy over them.

Popcorn

Bring two or three people up front, then have those who are seated "pop" up, at random, to be prophesied over by those up front.

Cell Phone

Have your group members pair off. Each person should think of someone who needs a word and would be likely to receive it. Taking turns, one of the partners should call the person they thought of and explain that he or she is participating in an activation session, and that his or her partner is going to pray over that person. Then, switch so that the other partners have a chance to do the same. Limit the phone calls to five minutes maximum.

Long-Distance

If you have several people in your class, call someone you know long-distance who may need a word. Make sure you arrange this in advance of your class so the person you call will be available and willing to have this done.

You can show a photograph of the person, or not. That's up to you. Don't offer any details about the person, but give the class the person's first name only. Have the recipient of the call say hello, and then begin.

With the phone on speaker, pass the phone around and have each student prophesy over the person. At the end, have the recipient offer feedback.

Mix It Up

Pair off and give each team of two a paper and pen. Have them take turns writing down something about their partner having to do with one of the following ten topics (or any topic of your choosing)—whatever comes to their spirit that seems to fit their partner in regard to the topic. Then have them share what they wrote with their partner.

+ cartoon character

+ actor/actress

+ singer

+ Bible character

+ color

+ number

+ Bible verse

+ historical figure

+ famous minister

+ song

These are just a few ideas. Make up some of your own and have fun exercising the gift!

ABOUT THE AUTHOR

Joni Ames is a single mother and grandmother who for twenty-five years served as administrative assistant for several well known ministries, including PTL, Jimmy Swaggart Sonlife Radio, CBN, Rick Joyner and MorningStar Ministries, and Derek Prince Ministries. She also served as Single Parents Leader for Central Church of God in Charlotte, North Carolina. She began her prophetic ministry through Women's Aglow and MorningStar Church in the 1990s. As ministry invitations increased, she eventually quit her full-time job and went on the road as the Lord opened the opportunity to do so. She has been in full-time ministry now for twenty-two years. Joni currently teaches and ministers prophetically to churches and ministry across the nation. Go to www.joniames.com for more information.

Welcome to Our House!

We Have a Special Gift for You

It is our privilege and pleasure to share in your love of Christian books. We are committed to bringing you authors and books that feed, challenge, and enrich your faith.

To show our appreciation, we invite you to sign up to receive a specially selected **Reader Appreciation Gift**, with our compliments. Just go to the Web address at the bottom of this page.

God bless you as you seek a deeper walk with Him!

WE HAVE A GIFT FOR YOU. VISIT:

whpub.me/nonfictionthx

WHITAKER
HOUSE